PASSING OF THE MILL VILLAGE

PASSING OF THE MILL VILLAGE

Revolution in a Southern Institution

———◆———

HARRIET L. HERRING

Research Associate, Institute for Research in Social Science
University of North Carolina

Chapel Hill
THE UNIVERSITY OF NORTH CAROLINA PRESS

Preface

THE sale of mill villages is clearly a movement of importance to a large part of the South. Its importance to the immediate locality of a sale is even clearer. No one is more aware of all this than the people who are a part of the movement. Whether they are directly concerned, like the employer who makes the decision to sell and the worker who buys, or indirectly like the school principal in the area and the casually observing citizen, they know something significant is going on. They view it with interest and talk about it with insight and understanding. I am grateful to hundreds of them for sharing with me their knowledge and observations; I am particularly indebted to mill managers and officials for taking time from busy schedules to discuss the ramifications of a complex subject and to round up for me such facts and figures as they could. Considering how long and often they have been "investigated," they are remarkably patient. For many of them this was only the latest of several calls I myself have made upon them for information and cooperation.

I wish to express for myself and for the Institute for Research in Social Science thanks to the Carnegie Foundation for the Advancement of Teaching for a grant through the University Research Council which made possible the travel necessary for the study, and to Mr. I. Rogosin of the Beaunit Mills, Inc., who offered, through Mr. Forrest Shuford of the North Carolina State Department of Labor, to assist in financing its publication. I am personally indebted to my colleagues of the Institute: to Gordon W. Blackwell, Director, who accepted the project with enthusiasm equal to my own; to Rupert B. Vance who used a sharp red pencil for minor changes and his usual force and logic in suggesting major revisions; to Katharine Jocher who edited the manuscript for publication.

H.L.H.

Chapel Hill
May, 1949

Table of Contents

PASSING OF THE MILL VILLAGE

CHAPTER I

Introduction: An Old Institution in a New Time

COTTON mills in the South are selling their villages. The movement began in a tentative sort of way during the mid-thirties and gained momentum until 1940. After the war it was resumed and is proceeding briskly. This development is startling because, of all industries which have resorted to company housing, in none has the custom been so general, of such long standing, and of so much public interest as in textiles. The reasons for the reversal of mill policy lie in the changes of the last two decades. The process presents an example of the break-up of an institution. If the movement continues the results will have social and economic significance for the entire Piedmont South.

The company-owned village has been a conspicuous adjunct of the cotton mill whenever and wherever this branch of textiles has sprung up. The reason is simple. Machinery was invented for spinning and weaving cotton well before that for any other important processing. In the factory system which machinery ushered in three elements were needed in abundance, capital, power, and labor. Before the day of electricity and railroads, power was the least mobile. The English mills were built at the rapids of rivers where there were few workers to be had from the sparse rural population. Operatives brought or attracted from elsewhere had no means with which to build homes, and investors in rental property had not yet found this new opening. The mills had to provide housing. When textiles rose as the pioneering factory in New England and the South the same conditions existed and the mills built villages as a matter of necessity and a matter of course.

In the other great mill areas, as the industry grew the villages were enlarged more slowly than the mill or not at all; presently they began to decline actually, and finally, well before the industry reached its peak, all but disappeared. In the South, for geographic, social and economic reasons, company housing for textile workers kept pace with the increase in mills until the middle 1920's at which time the industry reached its highest point in number of mills and, until the 40-hour two-shift week, in number of workers.

3

And so the cotton mill village has long been an important feature in the physical and social landscape of the South. The main outlines of the pattern were set before the Civil War by pioneering mills such as Saluda and Graniteville, South Carolina; Prattville, Alabama; Spray and Alamance, North Carolina; and many others: a few houses, a little school, a little church, a handful of families, and an owner-manager who ran the mill and community benevolently or otherwise according to his disposition. In the mill building era the pattern was repeated a thousand times, spread over the South for all to see. What Southerners saw looked good. Every phase represented an improvement over the lean and hungry past, and a promise of a fuller future: neat, "pleasantly uniform" cottages; rehabilitated people earning wages and creating profits; a community with the essentials of group living, such as school, church, and store; and best of all, an owner who took a fatherly interest in his people, protected them from the evils of drink by prohibiting saloons, eliminated "undesirables" from the community, helped the needy.

The first disapproval, beginning about 1900, was directed, not at the village, but at the mill for its child labor and long hours. Concern with these questions brought investigators, including "outside reformers," to look at the village. Within a decade they were describing it as feudalistic. They said the people were tied to the mill from infancy in swaddling clothes bought on credit at the company store to death followed by burial in the company cemetery. Presently critics, mostly non-southern, attacked the unsatisfactory physical conditions of the poorer villages; defenders, mostly Southerners, countered with descriptions of the growing welfare activities of the more progressive companies.

By the 1920's censure of the village was emphasizing its social and psychological aspects: controls as related to morals, absence of freedom of occupational choice, separatism of the village as a breeding ground of class and caste. The atmosphere surrounding the subject became so charged with controversy that a new group on the scene, students seeking to study and analyze, were classed with the pros if they said a word of good, with the cons if they saw the least flaw. As a result of almost continuous discussion, the southern mill village became far better known than its prototypes in other industries. The company town of an individual firm was often just as paternalistic, but it was an occasional phenomenon in its industry and its neighborhood. The lumber towns were usually far worse physically, but they were thought of as temporary. The coal mining towns were controlled with an iron hand, but they were out of sight in the hills, and, besides, their people were often immigrants and not the "purest Anglo-Saxon blood in America."

By contrast, the southern mill village has taken its place in the eyes of the Nation as one in a long procession of peculiar characteristics of the South, along with slavery and cotton, sharecropping and low incomes, race problems and demagogic Democracy. To the South it has become a sort of institution with an established set of accepted usages.

As an institution the southern mill village has had the sanction of long custom, even longer than its existence in the South. For despite differences in details, in its social and community features it still strongly resembles the industry-owned villages that were built around the rural mills of England and New England a hundred and fifty years ago. Perhaps because textiles are the oldest factory industry, and because early conditions were repeated in each new locale, ways of meeting them have become strongly traditional. Many features have continued because "that is the way the mill business is run." One of these "ways" was housing of employees in company-owned, low-rent, subsidized villages.

As an institution its acceptance in the South was assured by its consistency with the southern social and economic order. In many other areas and industries people came to be considered a sort of social class when they became industrial workers. In the southern mind the people who went to the mills were already a social class for whom factory—even cotton mill—employment was a step upward. The South wanted manufacturing—cotton manufacturing— for the profits and for the social betterment that work and wages would give underemployed and underprivileged people. Small wonder that the region accepted as wise the social as well as the economic activities of the leaders who provided the profits and the employment.

As an institution the company-owned villages in the South have had the practical authority of usefulness. Cotton mills have jobs for men and women, and in the early days for children, in about the same proportion in which they are available for work in families, so that investment in a house used to mean several workers for the mill. The people, largely tenant or mountain farmers, came to the mill without funds, and wages were low. They had neither the habits of, nor the capital for, home ownership, and they did have the habit of mobility. And so, as nothing else could have done, the company village furnished workers to the mills and housing to the workers. In the achievement of these essential needs the social by-product was communities with conflicting values: mobility versus controls; physical and community facilities usually beyond what the people themselves could have established, but created and operated outside the democratic process; a relatively high degree of community harmony and often of *esprit de corps* along with community monotony and community isolation.

But changes are now taking place. These are the result of other changes, some gradual, some precipitate. The development of urban and interurban transportation began to free New England mills from dependence on company houses in the 1880's; good roads and cheap automobiles began the process for the South two generations later. Better housing standards made the village increasingly expensive while federal legislation on wages made the growing expense a competitive disadvantage. Legislation protecting unionization efforts wiped out the most strategic of its controls. The 40-hour week made two shift operations practically necessary at a time when few mills, emerging from a long depression, had the money to build houses; anyhow they found they could get workers for the extra shift without adding a house to the village. Finally, a new generation of mill managers had largely replaced the generation of old mill owners. Efficiency of management was now more fashionable than the paternalism of ownership. Out of these conditions is emerging a new movement, the break-up of the village by sale of the houses.

If the sale of company houses is a measure of recent changes it is also a precursor of future changes. A good many mills have already sold and, by all indications, more are considering this step. If this movement continues it will mean the passing of the mill village as a self-contained community and as a social institution. Its passing will affect not only the mill workers who live in the houses but those who do not as well, in all a third of a million workers, and with their families, close to a million people in the Piedmont South. It will affect an old industry and the new unions, an old psychological complex and a new freedom. The results of this change in ownership will be felt in the towns around which the villages cluster and the counties in which they are officially "rural-nonfarm," and unofficially are often sizeable towns. This change will almost surely have repercussions in local and probably in some state politics. It is a revolution. In a less hectic era it would receive attention as such.

Will the movement continue? This writer ventures the opinion that it will. The purpose of the mill village was fulfilled a generation ago. It has lingered, as institutions do, until the inconveniences of a real break become less painful than those of continuing the established form. The villages of hundreds of mills are still going concerns. On the surface they are indistinguishable from those which managers decided to sell; fundamentally their basis of existence has been subject to the same modifications which led the sellers to their decision.

For managers pondering these changes in the times there are plenty of examples of how others have met them. Experience with sales and selling is now extensive and has been accumulating over a decade of widely diverse conditions. The textile industry is a highly competitive business, and within its own circle, highly imitative. When one mill "finds a good thing," whether it be fiber or fabric, a new machine or a new way of applying labor to machinery, others follow. In no field have the mills been more imitative than in matters relative to the village—witness the rise of welfare work and the shifts in form it has taken, the trend to varied cottages and streets curved to the lay of the land, the decline of the company store and the installation of water systems, to cite a few examples. Mill men all over the South are looking at the experience in selling villages. What they, assisted by alert real estate agents specializing in village sales, are learning is convincing more and more to join in the movement.

CHAPTER 2

Movement of Sales

THE separation of housing from mill operation began in a rather indirect way. For several years before the depression textiles had their own particular depression. A number of mills were unable to weather the increasing storms of the early 1930's. If the mill was completely liquidated, a purchaser of the mill building for other uses might not want the houses; if it was closed more or less indefinitely the firm might decide to realize on the houses and at the same time get itself out of the rental business. There was a market, of sorts, for the houses. The former employees already in the houses were potential purchasers if they had been able to find jobs in the neighborhood. In some cases the management or the receiver sold directly to as many as wished to buy, as well as to non-mill families. More convenient and more common were block sales to local investors. These were usually real estate dealers, and occasionally were men who had a financial interest in the mill and were helping to salvage something from an unfavorable situation. They rented the houses pending sale.

While this kind of sale was not included in this study, some 25 were encountered incidental to the search for regular sales with the mill continuing in operation. Half of them had taken place by 1933. In six more cases the houses were sold later though the mill had not been in operation since early depression days. All these were in North Carolina. That State has more spinning mills than its neighbors, a section of the industry specially hard hit by the depression. Also North Carolina had more companies owning only one or two plants. The larger firms here, as in the other States, were often able to retrench by closing a unit without having to sell either mill or dwellings. There may have been a few instances of similar sales in the other States of the South but they are believed to have been rare.[1]

Local authorities agreed that in these "depression" sales a large

---

1. Local informants cited this kind of sale when answering inquiries about those by operating companies, though they always made it clear that they distinguished between the two. In this way two such "incidental" sales were discovered in South Carolina which had taken place in the late 1930's.

proportion of the houses were bought by former employees of the mill, with few permanently entering the rental market. Their recollection that the transfers went on gradually was corroborated by an examination of the records in the offices of the Registers of Deeds. When improving business brought the reopening of such a mill, the owner—usually a new company—found available an experienced labor force in the former mill houses.

The intermediate step between the incidental separation of houses from mill and the deliberate policy of village sale was taken in the early 1930's by Burlington Mills Corporation, a growing producer of rayon fabrics. Rayon was not as hard hit by the depression as cotton, and so this company's greater regularity of operation and better wage scale made it possible to secure workers without providing houses. Some of its units operated in types of textiles, like full-fashioned hosiery and specialties, which had not customarily housed employees, or were situated in towns where such industries predominated so that the local labor supply already lived in their own or privately rented homes. With a keen entrepreneur at its head and a managerial group less strongly bound than usual by mill tradition, it had decided to concentrate its efforts on the manufacturing job. For much of its rapid expansion Burlington Mills bought cotton mills on the market because of the depression. Often it bought only the mill building, leaving the houses to be disposed of by the former owner in the manner just described. It was an easy step to sell a village the company may have reluctantly bought along with a mill building. Its first sales of two such villages in 1935 were so natural an extension of the company's policy that they attracted practically no attention.

The idea, however, of doing something about the village was in the air. Some thoughtful men in the industry had long felt, for reasons that will be discussed later, the need for modification of the housing system. But it had become so much a part of the whole complex set-up of investment, wages, employee relations, habits of the workers, and community responsibilities of the employer, that it was hard to see a way to break the long tradition. Then in 1933 discussion of the Textile Code under the National Recovery Act brought the idea sharply to the front. President Roosevelt suggested, as an addition to the Code, that the economic problem of regional wage differentials and the social problem of control be attacked at their roots by the mills disposing of their villages. A committee from the industry was appointed to study the subject.

Like individual mill men, the committee was overwhelmed by the complications involved in turning the villages loose. Its report boiled down to a baffled admission that it saw no practical way of separating housing from the mill. Writers in the trade papers were more resourceful; articles proposing various solutions appeared throughout the 1930's and included suggestions for putting houses and community business on a cost-of-service basis, or providing all workers with acreage for small farms.

Out of this search for a new solution to the village problem the one that seemed most practical was the one then going on, namely, sale, whether by mills closing or changing hands, or by an operating company ready to take the plunge. By the time the committee issued its report saying that separation was not feasible, the sales had already begun. At least one sale antedated those by Burlington Mills Corporation. In 1934, the Elmore Corporation at Spindale, North Carolina, sold its houses to the employees. This company was founded in 1920 with a small mill and some 30 houses. The Spindale area has grown rapidly in population with many textile workers building homes. The mill found it unnecessary to add houses when it was enlarged or even when it operated double shift under NIRA. The few houses furnished so small a proportion of the workers needed that the owner decided they were not worth the trouble. The sale created no more stir than the two by Burlington Mills the next year.

The latter company continued its policy in 1936 with four more sales at North Carolina and Virginia plants. In the same year individual mills in Gastonia, North Carolina and Spartanburg, South Carolina joined the procession. In 1937 four companies in North and South Carolina sold the villages of ten mills. The most active year was 1939 when a dozen companies sold some 30 villages. By this time it had become apparent, at least in textile circles, that something revolutionary was going on.

Except for the completion of sales started in 1939, the year 1940 saw a distinct lull. Problems of national defense were mounting, and the certainty of military need for textiles pointed toward three-shift operation with greatly increased labor needs. Such conditions discouraged any move that might decrease labor supply. As a result, many managements that had been considering sales abandoned the idea for the time being. Only five companies carried through sales in 1940-41, disposing of 14 villages. Certainly in the case of the largest company involved, and probably in the others, the policy had been decided well before.

By the time the war started, then, about 25 firms in Virginia, North Carolina, South Carolina, and Georgia had sold some 60 villages including a total of nearly 7,000 houses. There was only one sale during the war, though several concerns continued throughout the war years their program of selling one house at a time as the employee-occupant wanted to buy. As the war progressed new taxes were levied which bade fair to take a large slice of the proceeds of sales. Managers who referred to this subject differed in their interpretation of the tax laws. For example, one thought that if the value had been written off under depreciation schedules, only the 25 percent capital gains tax would have applied. Another was sure the receipts would have been subject to full excess-profits taxes. While this factor offered a further deterrent to village sales it by no means ranked with the uncertainty of the effect on labor supply.

Village sales were resumed immediately after the war. Three firms sold 12 villages in 1945, one group of sales continuing into 1946, when three more concerns joined in selling four villages. Most of these were in Georgia and Alabama, the latter State entering the procession for the first time. In 1947, seven companies sold 13 villages, and one of the seven sold another in early 1948. Sales of 31 villages by 14 companies during and since the war have totaled well over 5,000 houses.

The above figures represent the sales covered by this study. There have been others, including some going on at this writing. Locating sales some years ago was relatively easy because each had a news value well beyond its immediate neighborhood. Nowadays in areas where they have become common sometimes even mill managers may not have heard that a nearby village has been sold.

Any statement as to the percentage of mills that have sold their villages can be only an approximation. Not only is the count of sales incomplete, but much depends on the definition of what constitutes a sale, for instance, sale of part of a village. Also the total number of mills depends on what groups of textile establishments are included. The bases used are explained in more detail in Appendix I, p. 122. The table on p. 12 gives at least a rough idea of the extent to which the movement had progressed by early 1948.

More mills in North Carolina, both in actual numbers and per-centagewise, have sold their dwellings than in all the other southern States combined, and, as Table 1 shows, mills in North Carolina began to sell earlier. The reasons for this difference are complicated and indeed are not entirely clear. Discussion of some of the reasons is, perhaps, not out of place here. The same conditions which probably made selling start earlier and proceed faster in North Carolina

SALES OF MILL VILLAGES

PERIOD	VA.	N.C.	S.C.	GA.	ALA.		TOTALS
1934–41							
Included in Study	4	54	8	1	—	67	
Others	—	11	2	—	—	13	80
1942–early 1948*							
Included in Study	—	8	6	14	2	30	
Others	—	4	2	2	—	8	38
Mid-1948–Mid-1949							
Reported in Trade Papers .	—	6	3	—	—	9	9
Total Sales	4	83	21	17	2		127
Number of Mills, 1939** . . .	25	380	182	133	80		800
Percentage	16.0	21.8	11.5	12.8	2.5		15.9

*All except 5 sales (1 included in study and 4 others), actually from 1945 to early 1948.
**See Appendix I, p. 123, for classification of mills making up this total. Other southern States not added because no sale was discovered in those States.

have been developing in the other southern textile States and point to more and more village sales.

One reason for the greater number of sales is the fact that three North Carolina companies which decided to sell, controlled a large number of mills. Incidentally, the four sales in Virginia were conducted by two of the three companies referred to, and so on a policy basis really belong with the North Carolina sales. But the question then arises, what made them decide to sell while similar companies in other States sold none or only one or two of their villages.

The answer lies partly in the fact that North Carolina has several large industries that do not have villages. The tobacco and furniture industries have no tradition of housing. Hosiery mills, where the custom was never so strong as in cotton mills, have housed fewer and fewer people as the industry grew; in the rapid expansion of full-fashioned hosiery manufacturing after World War I, few of the new mills built any houses. These industries gave constant and enviable proof that it was possible to operate without owning villages. They have also served to build up a considerable industrial labor supply that is not dependent upon the employer, and the cotton mills were able to get some operatives from this supply.

A study made by the writer in the middle 1920's covered 322 mills in North Carolina. Among these, 50 were hosiery mills, 30 of which housed no workers, and the others housed less than a fourth of their employees. The 250 cotton mills reported were housing an over-all average of 70 percent of their employees. About a third of the 250 housed only half, and some individual mills far less than half. And this was in a period of one shift, with very occasional or partial two-shift operation. While comparable data for the other southern textile States are not available in as great detail, the general impression prevailed at the time that mills in South Carolina, Georgia, and Alabama on the average were housing a larger proportion, and that few failed to house well over half of their employees.

Most North Carolina mills that have sold had been housing less than half, and some as low as 10 percent of their working force, and this before the prevalence of three-shift operation. Most mills in the other States that have sold have been housing over half, in a good many instances 75 percent on a three-shift basis, and some as high as 90 percent on a two-shift basis.

Thus North Carolina mills have been for a longer time and to a larger extent employing people who housed themselves through ownership or rental. As will be noted in another connection, this fact was important in many decisions to sell. The North Carolina mills began 25 to 30 years ago to get workers from the adjacent towns, from privately owned houses on the fringe of the villages, and as roads and automobiles increased, from the countryside.

The relative importance in this State of the rural supply is apparent to the casual observer driving along the roads of the Piedmont South. In North Carolina the highways leading to industrial towns and cities are veritable "stringtowns"; in the other States one approaches many towns, even those with sizeable mills, through open fields after passing the marker for the beginning of the corporate limits. North Carolina started large-scale road building a little ahead of the neighboring States; by 1927 it had twice as much hard-surfaced mileage as Georgia and South Carolina and 50 percent more than Alabama. The plan of connecting all county seats gave many towns, by the late 1920's, a radiating system, and many others hard-surfaced roads in two directions. It is obvious from the style (or lack of style) of architecture that the vast majority of houses in these stringtowns have been built in the last 20 to 25 years, and many in the last decade. It is equally obvious that they are not farmhouses—lack of outbuildings and the size of the plots of land preclude anything except a garden or small-scale, part-time farming. It is perhaps significant that when the source of labor was being discussed with managers, those in North Carolina almost invariably said they drew from "the countryside for miles around," while those in South Carolina almost as invariably mentioned the towns within a radius of 20 to 30 miles as the source of non-company housed workers.

The mills that have sold their villages form a cross section of almost all of the differences shown by mills in the South. The 97 sales covered by this study represent 37 companies. In size they range from some of the largest in the region owning many mills to small companies with a single plant. In the case of about half of the firms and one-third of the sales, the ownership or control or both are clearly outside the South; some of the others may be indirectly controlled outside the South. Some companies, both southern and non-southern controlled, large and small, have plants with villages they definitely do not plan to sell. Some sold a number of villages in one large sale or a continuous series of sales; others have spaced the sales of different villages, while still others have sold the houses of a given village one or a few at a time over a period of years.

Mills that have sold run the entire gamut of textile products in the South. This means they represent a wide range of worker skills on the one hand and, on the other, different problems of stability of operation. These latter problems are rendered more diverse because of marketing systems that range all the way from those selling a staple semi-finished product through a commission house to others with parent companies taking their entire product, to still others selling consumer staples or specialties direct to the retail trade through their own highly organized sales department supported by national advertising.

The villages sold show great difference in location. Some are well inside city or small town limits or are suburban to such cities or towns. Others make up practically all the town, and still others are country villages. Some are in the midst of a textile area with the advantages to the mill of a large experienced labor force and the disadvantages of other employers competing for the labor of their erstwhile tenants. Others are well away from any other mills, with and without non-mill employment available, thus posing different combinations of advantage and disadvantage to the mill and the home-owning worker.

All this diversity is repeated in the type and condition of the houses and in the conduct of the sales. As will be shown in succeeding chapters, the details of the selling process differed widely as did the personnel relations and the community services. Many of these features can be covered only superficially in a survey of this kind. Detailed and continuous observations from the announcement of a sale through the years of adjustment to home ownership would be needed to make clear the modifications which take place in industrial relations and in family and community life. The social change implicit in this transition in an institution is worthy of such study. It would tell us much about labor-management relations, and about the growth and developing functions of communities, of responsible citizenship, and of democracy.

CHAPTER 3

The Decision to Sell

No single reason was found for sales in general or indeed even for a sale in particular. Rare indeed was the mill man interviewed in the course of this study who did not give several reasons for his own decision. Rarer still was there one who did not indicate his realization that, even if his chief reasons were simple and concrete, they grew out of long developing change.

The reasons given by mill managers can be summarized briefly. Those most frequently mentioned centered around cost: the desirability of stopping the subsidy for maintenance, the investment no longer necessary in order to secure labor, and the capital thus tied up needed for use in the mill itself. Allied to these, but somewhat less frequently cited were, on the one hand, the practical disappearance of regional differentials in wages which makes village expense a competitive disadvantage, and on the other, higher textile wages which make home purchase feasible. Other reasons centered more directly around the workers. One mentioned by nearly every manager was the unfairness of low mill rent to a part of the force, an injustice of which they were constantly reminded by the complaints of workers housing themselves at greater expense. Another represented the hope and belief that property owning would stabilize the workers and lessen labor turnover, and—the frank admission by a few—that it might also lessen interest in unions and strikes. Still another revealed a change in attitudes: that the paternalism of the mill village is no longer needed and indeed is coming to be resented. Running through all the reasons like a refrain was the conviction that home ownership would make for more responsible citizens and better communities.

For the reader unfamiliar with the economic, social, psychological, and technological changes involved in these reasons, some account of their development is perhaps appropriate.

When the mills first started in the South, either at isolated water power facilities or near towns, the necessity for housing could be met by the simplest of two or three room cottages. At low rents or none at all, fairly tight against the weather and often even painted, with a privy in the back yard and a deep well in every block, they represented an improvement over the former living conditions of the recruited operatives. The mills, the boosters for more mills, and the surrounding public had much to say about the rise in living standards which industry had brought to the people.

But a rise in a standard of living is a progressive thing. The people wanted larger cottages—three or four rooms instead of two or three, and after a while four or five rooms. And better cottages—ceiled and then plastered, running water taps on the porch, and presently inside toilets and baths. The paternalistic nature of the institution gave the owner a personal pride in having a sightly village. Also he thought that comfortable houses and presently welfare work and community activities would attract good workers and lessen their habit of moving.

Newer villages started with these better features and most of the older ones were refurbished to keep them from being too far behind. All this went on over a period of generally profitable operation which made the improvements possible. But it was also a period of rising costs, reaching a climax just after the first World War when the kind of houses it was fashionable to build were costing as much per room as they used to cost per house. In addition there was the expense of water and sewer lines, of graded, sand clay and sometimes paved streets.

And yet the low or even nominal rents continued, with electricity in all the houses and water in an increasing number either free with rent or at similar nominal charges. During the middle 1920's, the writer, collecting data on company housing, had figures presented at hundreds of mills to show the deficit between rental returns and costs, and comparisons with private rents in the vicinity at two to four times as great. When asked why they did not increase the rents to cover the cost of the service the reply was: "It has always been customary to charge low rents"; or "The other mills charge these rates, the workers are used to it and would not like it if we charged more." The tradition, then as earlier, was reinforced by a strong but less often expressed reason, namely, low wages. By the middle 1920's most of the wage increases of World War I had melted away under the pressure of competition in an overdeveloped industry and in the presence of a plentiful labor supply. Low rent was a form of wage supplement and, even at a deficit, was cheaper in wholesale housing than in wage increases.

But the discouraging thing was that for all the improvement, the enlarged community services and the increased costs, the mill village was getting a "bad" name. When housing was simpler and cheaper and community welfare largely the personal activity of the officials, the mills were generally praised for what they did with only an occasional discordant note of criticism, and that usually from an "outsider." By the 1920's they were quite generally criticized, even by a good many Southerners. The emphasis of criticism was gradually shifted from physical conditions to the social and economic controls inherent in the company village. Efforts to organize labor in 1928-1930 brought these controls into active play as individual managements sought to prevent unionization by keeping agitators out and by getting rid of employees who embraced a trouble-making cause. The inconsistencies of these methods with the benefits claimed for paternalism caused the latter term and its manifestations to deteriorate in esteem. Some workers had registered their lack of interest in or actual dislike for welfare activities merely by not taking part in them; as their education by organizers proceeded they began asking why the money was not put in the pay envelopes instead. For this reason and for lack of funds, this period saw a decline in welfare work.

In this same period other conditions were affecting the supply and demand for labor. By the middle 1920's mill expansion had temporarily ceased in the old textile States from Virginia to Alabama, and a little later job re-alignment, the famous "stretch-out," made fewer workers necessary. Agricultural prices were declining and, as roads and automobiles made it convenient, a member or two of many families drove in from nearby farms to supplement their incomes with a cash wage. As textile wages declined or work became irregular, some mill families moved to the country in order to make ends meet by doing a little farming on the side. The mills found that in temporarily busy times these sources provided plenty of labor.

Owners and managers who were no longer housing most of the workers began to see disadvantages of a new sort in the village. Workers paying several times the mill rate of rent to private landlords complained and pressed their application for mill houses. Though many workers bought homes, others refrained because it was poor business as long as they could get houses at less-than-cost rental rates. Workers who did buy paid for their thriftiness by higher housing costs, and sometimes one would try to get the mill to purchase from him and rent back to him at the regular mill rate.

The depression accentuated all these conditions that had been developing for a decade. And it brought the New Deal. The National Recovery Act sought to shorten hours so that more people would be employed, to raise wages and decrease regional differentials, and to protect the workers in their efforts at unionization. All these features struck at the roots of the mill village. While NRA did not succeed in equalizing New England and southern textile wages, it reduced the differential and brought into the open the only legitimate excuse for it, namely, such perquisites as low-cost housing and community services. Emerging tentatively from a long depression few mills had the money, if they had the inclination, to enlarge their villages to house a second and a third shift; with the 40-hour week at least two shifts were a practical necessity to spread overhead costs. The eagerness for employment brought the workers, and so was dispelled the illusion that company housing was a necessity.

Labor organizers took advantage of the protection of the new law and the dissatisfaction over the stretch-out to conduct a whirlwind evangelistic campaign by preaching on the text, "President Roosevelt wants you to organize." Apprehensive as to just what the law would do to them, the mills were hesitant about using to the full the time-tested methods of all employers, especially those with company villages, for discouraging unions. The textile strike of 1934, although unsuccessful because of bad timing, poor strategy, and lack of a solid grounding of the workers in unionism, was large enough and widespread enough to show what protection for the right to organize might do.

Several acts filled in the vacuum when NRA was declared unconstitutional. The National Labor Relations Act went further than NRA in protecting the right to organize. Its Administrative Board went further still: in complaints from employees endeavoring to organize, the very ownership of a village—because of the reputation of company towns in general and the southern mill village in particular, together with the general bent of its staff—made the Board assume that controls had been exercised. Housing had become a strategic liability. One manager said quite frankly he thought the mill would be better off without a village if it had a case before the NLRB.

The Wage Hour Law confirmed the short work week, decreased differentials, and provided for periodically increased minimum wages. With better wages the workers were able to pay more rent. But the Wage Hour Board's rules about deductions for goods and services limited possible increases on the one hand, and on the other restricted rental charges to a low return on investment less depreciation. Many of the villages were old enough to have had the original cost written off.

The two-shift operation and increased business uncovered, even before the war, a shortage of experienced workers. During its depressed condition in the late 1920's and early 1930's the industry had trained relatively few new operatives, and the new arrangement of jobs and faster machines were enabling it to make more effective use of skilled workers by giving them unskilled assistants. The new laws regulating the wages of learners made large-scale training expensive and increased the value of experienced labor. The individual manager felt that any considerable raise in rents would put his mill at a disadvantage in holding such workers unless all the rest conformed. Some increased rents from twenty-five cents to fifty cents a room a week but rising maintenance costs largely nullified its modest effect. Many managers interviewed in 1947-1948 had kept the same rental rates and gave the same reasons of custom which they or their predecessors had given two decades before. This time they often added, "We should have charged more," or "We are suckers." These low rents made a mill house more and more desirable as the housing shortage developed and private rents were raised. The complaints of non-housed workers and their charges that there was partiality in assigning the houses were, in many instances, an important reason for the sale.

One local manager who had opposed the sale decided upon by the parent company thought a better policy would be to provide good houses, keep them in tip-top condition, and charge rents to cover the cost. Several others said this would not work: If employees were paying high rents they would expect of the mill far more in upkeep, painting and the like than they do for similar rates from private landlords; the messy tenant would be forever demanding attention and the good one would feel that care and cleanliness were poorly rewarded. "The mill couldn't charge enough to cover it," they said.

All the while the mills have been getting fewer workers from a given number of houses. In the old days the rule, enforced by the mill's need for workers or the family's need for wages, had been a worker per room. Child labor laws had gradually reduced this. By the middle 1920's the average was one-half a worker per room. The rising standard of living that made a family want a larger house was paralleled by a decrease in the size of mill families. Few now have the six, eight, ten children common in the mountain and tenant farm families drawn to the mills 50 or even 30 years ago. During National Recovery days better wages relieved the pressure on mothers to work and enabled young people to continue in school beyond the legal working age. By 1940 a mill did well to average three-tenths of a worker per room, or only slightly better than one worker from a four-room house. The expense of the village was less and less justified by the labor supply it provided.

These changes—legal, economic, and social—have been accompanied by managerial and technological change in the last two decades. The new system of applying labor to machinery, which at its worst was the stretch-out and at its best a long-delayed and logical modernization in job alignment, requires more attention to wage scales and rates and to industrial relations than the old, rather casual ways. Improvements in machines and new fibers and fabrics during the decade before World War II made many mills obsolescent. The new processes are making textile manufacturing more and more complicated, requiring alertness on the part of the management aided by a staff of technical specialists. Government rules and regulations during the New Deal and the war period required much attention and have by no means ended. It is not strange that some managements felt the manufacturing job made sufficient demands on their time and money without investment in housing and attention to the problems involved in a village.

Among the most interesting reasons given for selling the villages were those involving paternalism and home ownership because they represent a change of attitude growing out of changed conditions. In the 1920's, although criticisms of the mill village and of paternalism were at a high pitch, mill men were either on the defensive or quite honestly proud of both. Literally hundreds of them told the writer then that they "took care of their people"; or that the village was quite complete as to school, church, recreation, relief, everything, and the people preferred not to mix with those of the adjoining town; that the people expected the mill to keep up the moral tone of the village by refusing to hire or to retain undesirable families in the community; that the people did not want the responsibility, the expense or the loss of mobility involved in home ownership—a dozen ways of saying they thought the system was good and the people thought so too. The opinion on this subject, at least on the part of those who have sold villages, is now quite different. They know, and will now say, that many workers do not like paternalism and that it is a healthy sign that they do not: "They want to stand on their own feet just like anybody else; the mill is paying and should pay wages that make this possible." Some of these men have become convinced that the mill cannot make better citizens of the workers, that the people become better citizens only by encountering the responsibilities of full citizenship.

There are, of course, many special circumstances which add their weight to the general conditions discussed above and swing the decision in favor of selling by an individual company. One manager who sold several years before the war boom period said the desirability of securing the money invested in the houses to retire preferred stock and place the company in a stronger financial position was an important factor. Another selling about the same time said his small mill had barely been able to keep afloat during the depression so that the income from the payments along with the stopping of maintenance costs made considerable difference in its position. Several made the sale to secure capital for long delayed modernization, and the decision paid off well in the war period of heavy operation and inability to get machinery. Surprisingly enough, one manager who sold since the war said the reason was partly because the mill needed the money. It was installing new machinery at the time of the sale.

At another post-war sale the manager said that some ten years earlier a number of his employees bought land ranging from large lots to several acres in a new development a few miles away and built houses. It was observed that this group made the best workers, cooperative, stable and steady—"seemed to want to get somewhere." This object lesson helped in the decision to sell. Still another cited a small problem which added its bit of weight: his village was "getting to have right many" houses occupied by elderly people and furnishing no workers at all. The mill needed the houses but naturally found it difficult to get old, long-service people out. At the sale their options were taken by one or another of their children.

There probably were many other special reasons; although most of the mill men were frank and cooperative, they were under no obligation to go into every circumstance with an investigator. In most localities people with varied sorts of contacts with the former village were interviewed for their observation of the processes and results. In several cases these outsiders, and in a few cases union officials, offered the opinion that the mill sold because it anticipated or was already in difficulties with the union.

Location was sometimes the determining factor: the same management would sell the village belonging to one or more units of the company and retain those at others. They felt that their isolated mill would be at a disadvantage in attracting workers if they did not have houses to offer, since it was certain that at least some of the workers would find other employment when they were no longer under obligation to work in the mill. One or two added that it was unfair to the workers to ask them to invest in a house where employment depended on one company. On the other hand, a few that were not near other mills sold their houses, conscious of the advantage of having workers anchored to the spot.

At least three who have sold recently were at the same time building houses. Other mill men labeled as a strange and illogical procedure this selling houses at low prices and building more at current high costs. The managers concerned found no paradox in this. The old houses had been largely or completely depreciated, justifying the low price at which they were sold. They felt that from their location, wage scale, and industrial relations they would retain most of the new home owners, and this is proving to be true. The severe housing shortage was making it difficult to secure workers, especially key men, who could not afford to build houses for themselves at present costs. To these reasons the managers might have added that the company could afford to do so since it had earned dollars in the same inflated market which made the new houses expensive. A manager who came to his company after the sale greatly regretted not having the houses during the war years and was unenthusiastic about sales in general. And yet he said that if he were building a new mill he would not include dwellings because that would tie up too much of a company's capital.

A few have sold rather hastily but most have looked into the experience of older sales, and in view of that knowledge have examined their own situation thoroughly before making the decision. For some this study has extended over several years and included such vital matters as village costs over a long period, their own history and prospects for stability, their relation to a parent company, the surrounding labor supply and competing employment in relation to their own wage scale and working conditions. When asked what would be their advice to other companies considering a sale, they almost invariably responded, "Study their own situation."

CHAPTER 4

Process of Selling: Preparation

THE process of selling a village involves many matters of policy and procedure. There have been almost as many variations in what and how to sell as there have been sales.

In most cases the mill has retained business property, though one or two sold that as well. The few mills which had substantial apartment houses held these. Some sold and others retained large boarding houses. In prewar sales some of the mills which had greatly reduced their welfare work sold buildings formerly used as community houses. A number of these were modified dwellings; one or two were large buildings which the purchasers (usually not employees) converted into multiple family houses. One group of mills sold a large community building which contained a gymnasium and swimming pool, and it has been used since as a garment factory.

One or two which owned churches or had a large equity in them gave them to the congregation or sold at nominal rates. Most of those which had been renting parsonages sold them to the churches at somewhat less than regular prices, though one mill retained two parsonages for rent. Several which owned the school building turned it over to the town or the county, some with and some without any payment. In at least one case the money received for the building was then given for the addition of a new department to the school.

Nearly all mills covered by this study retained at least the superintendent's house and a few for foremen and other key personnel. Some illustrative proportions kept are: 8 out of 300; 9 out of 240; 10 out of 240; 11 out of 205; 20 out of 190; 20 out of 210. One mill retained 110 out of its 550 houses so as to have some houses for loom fixers as well as foremen and assistant foremen.

A few mills have, for various reasons, retained an even larger proportion of their houses. One company still owns half the houses in its four villages. Its sale was started in 1939 and proceeded gradually without any definite time limit. By early 1940 sales had slowed up since most occupants who wanted to buy had done so. With the changing business outlook the management decided the remaining houses would be useful in a labor shortage and the sale was discontinued. Another company sold a block of 87 out of its 622 houses in 1941 as an experiment, but, as in the case cited above, decided against going further for the time being. Nor did it resume sales after the war.[1] In a postwar sale the company disposed of a section of the village which had a good dividing line from the rest, 40 percent of some 450 houses, also as an experiment, and will observe the effects before continuing sales there or at its other mills.

One company retained a few houses at its two villages and another about a third of its small village in order to have the land for possible expansion of mill, warehouse, and yard. Similarly, several retained a few houses where the space would obviously be needed for stores and other service expansion. These managements reasoned that a price approximating its real value would have made its purchase too heavy a burden for a family, while a price no higher than the other houses would have raised criticism from buyers less favorably located. In at least one case the occupant of such a house was offered the opportunity to buy another and he gladly took it. In one case, and there may have been others, the mill retained a house because a water tank was located on the lot.

In prewar sales the majority of the managers who had reserved very few or no houses said this had been a mistake. The draft and brisk business with offers to experienced key men caused considerable war-time turnover of some of the most valuable men in the mills. Very occasionally such a man who had bought a mill house sold to the one taking his place, but in the housing shortage, he usually had relatives or friends eager to get it. At least three mills bought back some of the houses at three and four times the sale price in order to have places for foremen; other mills were hard put to it to find quarters for replacements or additional foremen, mechanics, and in a few cases superintendents. One large company which shifted several plant managers and superintendents from place to place had sufficient *esprit de corps* for these men to swap houses fairly happily, but of course they were staying on with the company and each benefited by having a house. One small company had no regrets over selling foremen's houses; nearly seven years after the sale every home-purchasing foreman was still with the organization and the company was building a few foremen's houses as part of a mill expansion program.

In the few postwar sales where none of the houses had been retained there has been neither time nor the pressure for men to make

---

1. Latest news from the community is that it has begun to sell again.

this a vital problem. Several managers who commented on this point felt that in normal times it might not be essential to retain any, though most seemed to think it would be desirable.

REPAIR

In about three-fourths of the villages that have been sold the houses needed repairs: in prewar sales because minimum repairs had been carried on during the depression; in those immediately after the war, because of lack of material and labor.

In a fourth of the villages the houses were given a more or less thorough going over for repairs, about one-half prewar and one-half postwar sales. In nearly another fourth, mostly prewar, some individual houses were repaired, the agent being allowed to promise certain repairs in discussing its purchase with an occupant. In some cases the refurbishing was rather superficial and consisted mainly of painting the outside. In others, the houses were painted inside and out, reroofed entirely or roofs mended, floors, porches and steps repaired, and sills relaid where necessary.

In the case of several mills which changed hands the new owner made extensive repairs to run-down villages before selling. In a prewar sale, for example, the new company painted and repaired the houses, put in water and sewerage systems, and paved the streets. Detailed figures were not available, but the manager admitted that the houses, sold at prewar low prices, did not bring enough to pay for the water and sewerage installations. In a small postwar sale the new company spent on the village it had bought a year before, one-third as much as the houses brought.

One group of mills in the middle 1930's raised rents from the traditional twenty-five cents a room a week to fifty cents, promising to put all the increase back into the houses. This would have provided, on the average four-room house, about $50 a year. The company did a little better than its promise, since its repairs for the four years averaged $250 per house. The reconditioning amounted to 28 percent of the average price which was $885. A mill which sold soon after the war ended got the full psychological value for its repairs; it announced two years earlier that it was going to sell and began making all repairs possible under war conditions and finished up during and immediately after the sale. At the other extreme was a mill being operated by receivers at the time of the sale in the late 1930's, where the cost of repairs was added to the price, which was already fairly high compared to prices at contemporary sales. The purchasers could have done much of this repair work themselves and at less cash outlay.

In about half the sales the houses were sold as they stood. In some twenty villages they had been kept in good condition by routine repair; in about the same number they were in need of repairs. Where repairs had not been made recently or were not part of the bargain, prices were set with these needs in mind. At least that was the theory; as will be seen in a later discussion of prices, the general level for a village in need of over-all repair was often little different from one in good condition.

SURVEY

Only a few of the mills that have sold owned any houses scattered among those of private owners or other mills. Therefore, few houses had property lines that had been surveyed. The land for a mill village was customarily bought by the acre, and the houses built at any one time were usually spaced to allow all approximately the same sized lot. In preparation for a sale a survey has to be made to establish lines and secure data for deeds to the individual plots.

In most surveys the informal lines already acknowledged by usage and common sense—half way between houses—were those set. In one sale the manager said that since the spaces were large an extra lot had been laid off between many houses. A union worker interviewed said the lines were run practically under the eaves of each house thus making a "vacant lot" of what had always been considered side yards of two houses. The new owners were not only indignant at the deal itself but uneasy lest the mill or some purchaser squeeze another house in the space. This particular sale was apparently unhappy in some other respects as well.

Fortunately this sort of difficulty seems to have been rare. At the other extreme was a village where about half the houses were so situated that each could have a narrow but deep lot of approximately an acre of land. The mill had some vacant land adjoining the village, and this was subdivided and assigned to the houses with small lots in order to give each purchaser as nearly an acre as possible. Other mills have not carried this strong tradition of "treating all the workers alike" quite so far. They have accounted for the difference in size of lots by difference in price and have laid out bona fide vacant lots in the village or divided up extra land at its edges into plots which they sell to employees who had no opportunity to buy a mill house and who wish to build a home.

SELLING AGENT

In half a dozen of the sales covered by this study the mills sold direct to the employees, managing the whole operation in their regular offices. In a dozen more the person or persons assigned to the job were assisted by a local lawyer, a real estate or building and loan man experienced in the details of such transfers. These were sometimes with and sometimes without a temporary office set up for the purpose. Roughly a dozen more turned the sale over to a local agency, a real estate company or building and loan association. In some of these the temporary selling office was at the mill; other managers thought it was better psychology for the purchasers to go to the downtown office of the agent.

In 60 percent of the sales the company has employed an outside selling agent to handle the whole matter. There are now several real estate or investment companies in the Piedmont South which have specialized in mill village selling, two of them quite large. Such agents are prepared to adapt their services to the wishes of the company and to advise on policy and procedure. They have experienced staffs to help with the survey, with appraisals and price setting, to explain terms to buyers at a temporary office in the village and by visits to the homes; they collect down payments and work out weekly or monthly installment scales to fit the desired payment period and the prices of the houses; and arrange for future payments as the mill prefers. If the mill does not wish to hold the mortgages they help arrange with local financial institutions to take them over, one of the companies being prepared to sell the mortgages to local or non-local banks.

Four companies disposing of 16 villages sold the whole property to outside parties who agreed to resell according to prices and priorities specified by the mill. In the largest company the new owners then employed one of the agents specializing in selling villages; the other purchasers, being real estate agents, ran their own sales.

This investigator did not press questions as to commission rates but it was volunteered in a number of cases. The usual commission seems to be 5 percent, with 3 percent on all over $1,000,000.00 A few have been a little above 5 percent and a few only 3 percent on the entire sale.

APPRAISAL

Appraisals have been made in all sorts of ways. In two cases an official of the company made the appraisals and set the prices entirely by himself, and indeed did the selling as well. These were small companies and each man had spent a lifetime in the mill, knew the workers personally and had their confidence. Other mills which did their own selling had a local contractor, a real estate dealer or building and loan representative make, or assist in making, appraisals. Where an agency experienced in selling villages is employed, its representatives usually make appraisals, though most mills have one or more of their officials and sometimes a local real estate man help also in setting the prices. The manager of one company said the mill made no suggestions and accepted without revision the prices set by representatives of the local real estate board. He announced this fact to the potential purchasers as he considered it a good technical point, showing the employees that the prices had been arrived at by competent and impartial judges unaffected by the mill's ideas. Few went so far as this in keeping hands off, but so far as was disclosed, only one went as far in the other direction as the company which exactly halved the prices set by the outside selling agent aided by local appraisers. Another set the prices at 60 percent of those suggested by local real estate appraisers, and still another at 66 percent of the outside specialists' prices.

In arriving at differentials among houses, appraisers took into consideration the usual items such as size and condition of the house, size and contours of the lot, and location. In all except the last item the ordinary standards are applicable and demonstrable. Location has some special features which the working man sees in a different light from the real estate appraiser. He probably finds nearness to work more than overbalances a somewhat bleak outlook on, say, a mill warehouse; he objects to the extra cost when the appraiser thinks business may move that way and increase values; he is buying because he has to, and at the time of the sale, anyhow, is much more interested in price than in speculative values.

Since a mill village is by definition a residential area for working people of more or less similar status there are not the subtle differences in values based on social ideas of a desirable place to live common in ordinary towns. There are three exceptions to this generalization. First, the foreman's houses are usually grouped together, but, as they are usually larger and better built and on literally "better" streets, difference in price is acceptable for physical reasons; the social status is official and recognized as such. Secondly, the houses nearest to the mill entrance and office, usually also convenient to stores, post office, movies and the like are considered the most desirable in the village, and older residents work toward them as vacancies occur. But again a higher value has physical justification.

Thirdly, there is an area in most villages where it is not so desirable to live. In a scattered village this is some hollow or hill; in the average, compact, continuous village it is the last street. This is where the newer families are concentrated as the older, more stable employees seize opportunities to move nearer the desirable center. This area is often less well kept, critics say because it is out of sight of most visitors, and mill men say because the predominance of the transient type makes upkeep and such amenities as shrubbery difficult to establish and maintain. While this factor in price setting did not arise in every interview, it was mentioned often enough to confirm the writer's own knowledge of mill village life. One manager volunteered a striking example. His village consisted of an older part with uniform double houses on small lots, and an encircling "back street," of relatively new, single bungalows on large level lots, well planted and with a pleasant outlook. The prices set acknowledged the existing "social desirability" by valuing them at less per room than the older houses.

Usually the price is set quite definitely, house by house, though in some sales modifications were made in individual cases where a buyer was particularly insistent that the price of his house was out of line with that of others. In such cases still another appraiser is often brought in. In a few instances prospective buyers, dissatisfied with the price, brought in appraisers of their own. The figures suggested were higher than the mill prices and that settled the discussion. In a sale conducted by the mill with only a local lawyer-real estate man to handle technical and detail work, the two top officials saw most of the purchasers, specially those who were dissatisfied with announced prices, and, after some jockeying and "horse trading," arrived at a satisfactory figure.

Such price modifications are troublesome and time consuming when literally hundreds of houses are being sold. But managers who mentioned this as a feature of their sales felt it was worth the trouble. The danger of opening up all prices for discussion or of dissatisfaction on the part of those whose prices were not "adjusted" was more than overbalanced by the general psychological effect; the employees could see that the plan was not completely arbitrary and had room for the correction of errors in appraising.

All this sort of adjustment had to do with the price of one house in relation to that of another. There were sales, as will be noted later, where the whole scale was greeted at first as "mighty high," and a few where this feeling persisted. This investigator discovered only one case where there was an effective demand for a general reduction. There a strong union opposed the sale at every point that a resourceful leadership could think of and succeeded in getting the mill to agree to a 20 percent reduction in all prices.

The price level from which differentials for individual houses vary up or down is theoretically based on some sort of general principle. In some, cost less varying percentages for depreciation was used, but not too realistically since the villages were often old enough to have been written off the books at any normal depreciation rate. One or two used some percentage of the tax valuation of the village as a basis for the total amount that they should receive and adjusted prices for individual houses around an average that would produce it. One company used 80 percent and another 75 percent of the fire insurance valuation in the same way. Some used a percentage of the replacement cost, 50 to 70 percent being the proportions mentioned in prewar sales. In both prewar and postwar sales a basis used was some percentage of the sales value compared with current prices for similar houses in the vicinity, 50 percent, 66 percent, and 75 percent being mentioned. Some, apparently, accept the general price level suggested by specialized selling agents who compare the village with others they have sold recently. In a postwar sale the basis used was one-half the cost of houses the company was then building at another mill. The manager added later a fact which may have been a factor in deciding: the total return was approximately the amount apportioned to village value when the company bought the entire property during the war.

These different bases represent a search for a general price level that would be, as was often expressed, "fair," "acceptable to the employees," "a generous price," and most of all, what they can afford to pay. In fact three managers volunteered this last as the really controlling element and others intimated as much when discussing payment rates.

If a management has weighed all the general conditions and its own special situation and has decided it is wise to sell, it is going to sell. The money return is often less important than other considerations. In one large group of sales before the war, where the necessity to buy was not quite as pressing on the occupant as in postwar sales, the management said its very low price level was set to overcome any sales resistance. On the one hand it wanted to get rid of the houses and on the other it wanted as many workers as possible to join its already heavy sprinkling of home-owning employees. Several managers said that they considered prices which made the houses obvious bargains a good piece of industrial relations. Two, more outspoken or more thoroughly convinced of the wisdom of selling than usual, declared that a mill would be better off without a village if it had to give the houses away; that the subsidy saved would equal the price in a few years, while freedom from all the headaches was an extra benefit.

PRICES

In terms of dollars these various bases, whether actually or only nominally used, and the resulting prices changed quite radically during the war. Therefore, discussion of actual prices is necessarily on two levels.

Prewar. Prices in sales from 1934 to 1941 ranged from $200 or $300 for a few very small, old cottages to around $2,000 for the largest and best, the latter an excellent type of house built by some mills for their foremen. Examples of price ranges in individual pre-war sales are as follows: $650 to $1,300; $600 to $1,500; $850 to $1,500; $200 to $1,400; $595 to $1,750; $700 to $1,400; $750 to $1,075; $750 to $1,100. Most managers said they had few in either of the extreme figures. The vast majority of houses were priced between $800 and $1,000. Nearly all villages had a few three-room, and a few five and six-room houses, with an average of about four rooms. Not many villages sold before the war had any double houses. The over-all average in 41 villages for which data are available was $920, or about $230 per room. This covers 4,200 houses.

Postwar. Prices in sales since the war have ranged from $900 to $7,000. Several villages had a few old three-room houses which were priced from $900 to $1,050. One company had some eight-room double houses that were priced from $6,000 to $7,000, partly because of size and good condition and partly because of their location near a growing business district. Some examples of price ranges in individual sales are as follows: $900 to $3,600; $2,500 to $7,000; $1,050 to $1,500; $900 to $3,500; $2,000 to $3,500; $1,060 to $1,900; $1,300 to $2,300. The prices of the majority of the houses fell between $1,600 and $2,400. Prices per room ranged from $300 to $700 with the average in many sales falling between $400 and $500. The average per room for 20 villages and nearly 4,000 houses was $468. In six other villages sold since the war the range was so great due to type of house, location, or condition that the average was meaningless.

NOTICE OF SALES

In nearly three-fourths of the sales the company sent notices to occupants of the houses it proposed to sell. These letters stated the new policy; offered the house to the occupant, adding that it could be paid for in installments; directed him when and where to make inquiry as to prices and terms. In more than half of the sales, the company gave him a definite period in which to come to a decision, after which the house would be offered to other buyers, employees first and then outsiders. These letters of announcement usually included some remarks about the virtues and values of home ownership and the opportunity which the company was offering its workers.

In the remaining sales announcement was made variously: in one, two years ahead and in another several months ahead; in one as soon as the decision was made and when the survey and other preparations were started; in three or four the superintendent or some official of the company called in a few leaders in the community and told them of the new policy in general terms; in two companies selling four villages an official selected an employee he knew to be interested in home owning, offered him his house and let the word spread that others could buy if they liked. One company called employees together in the community house and the local real estate man in charge of the sale told them about it.

A time limit of 30 days in which to decide and "sign up" for the house is the general rule when specialized agents are employed, though there have been a few instances where it was longer or was not strictly adhered to. Such a limit is also common when local agencies operate the sale. Mills managing their own sales usually have less definite time limits or none at all. Some of the earliest to sell disposed of the houses over a period of a year, the sales proceeding slowly at first but accelerating as more employees decided to buy. One large mill planned to sell in batches of 50 houses at a time a few months apart. After several of these batches were disposed of the plan was changed to a faster rate.

CHAPTER 5

Process of Selling: Conditions of Purchase

PREPARATIONS for selling include the necessity of working out beforehand many policy details, terms, and other matters besides those discussed in the preceding chapter. These preparations become manifest to the tenants as conditions of purchase.

PREFERENCE AND PRIORITY

The policy of every company whose sale is covered by this study —and all heard of in any detail—has been to give the occupant of a house the option to buy it. When there is a definite time limit to the sale, which was true in well over half the cases, if he does not signify his desire to purchase within that period the house is available to some other employee. In the case of double houses preference went to the occupant with longer tenancy in that house irrespective of tenancy in other mill houses or employment service. If he does not wish to buy, the other occupant is given preference before it is available to other employees. Only a dozen of the villages covered by this study contained any double houses, the proportion ranging from 6 percent to 20 percent of the dwellings in those villages. All except 5 of the dozen were small or medium-sized villages, and so the proportion of double houses in all sales has probably been only 2 or 3 percent. In most sales, arrangements arrived at between occupants to exchange options take precedence over applications by nonoccupant employees.

But in keeping with the variety in all other respects, even such a simple rule as this had some modifications and exceptions. Several managers said a few occupants were not offered their houses: "I knew they would not want to buy and would not make good home owners"; "We tried to avoid selling to people who wouldn't keep their premises clean"; "They were not very desirable citizens and we did not want to make them a permanent part of the community." When asked how the occupants concerned reacted to this difference in treatment the reply was, "They knew why they weren't offered the house—didn't say a thing about it," or "One man asked and when told the reason he said frankly: 'Well, I didn't think I'd be allowed to get in on this.' " While this kind of exception was mentioned chiefly at small or medium-sized plants where the policy-setting officials knew most of the workers personally, it was also referred to in the sale of a large group of mills. Here the superintendents knew the families well enough to make the exceptions.

The percentage of occupants who took up the options was overwhelming, ranging from 80 to 100 percent with most above 90 percent. Usually other employees take the balance. Since no mill that has sold was housing all its employees there were plenty of potential employee-applicants. One large group of mills that had housed 75 percent of its workers had houses enough refused by occupants to supply all others who applied. A medium-sized company housing 48 percent could have sold 50 more than the 300 odd it had to dispose of, while one small mill which sold less than 100 houses was unable to satisfy 69 employee applications. In several postwar sales the occupants bought 100 percent, leaving none for other employees.

In a few prewar sales an occasional house not taken by occupant or non-housed employee for a home was sold to an employee for investment. In at least one case two or three bought by the superintendent proved very handy for housing key men in the war rush. In 20 prewar sales a house or two was sold to a local tradesman or mechanic who wanted to live near his store or shop. Such sales were usually passed upon by the superintendent or other official.

In less than a dozen villages were any houses sold to non-employees for rental purposes. The total number of such houses has been well under 1 percent of all houses disposed of in village sales. The circumstances of sales for rental are of interest. In a sale in 1936 involving 100 houses, about 15 percent were not taken by employees and these went to outsiders for rental purposes. The housing shortage was not severe in the vicinity and the houses were not very desirable, though their location was good. In another prewar case the company selling a number of villages ended the sale with 4 percent of the houses not taken by employees. As a community service several local businessmen formed a corporation to buy, rent, and eventually sell them. Within three years they had disposed of all, chiefly to employees of the mills, and at prices only $200 to $400 more than they paid. In view of the fact that the original price had been low, that both wages and prices were rising rapidly, employment greater and housing scarcer, this modest profit indicated either a great deal of public spirit on the part of the group or an understanding with the company that they would give employees who had been slow in deciding a chance to own their homes.

In two postwar sales around 10 percent of the houses were closed out to outsiders for rental purposes. In one instance poor industrial relations seem to have dampened employee enthusiasm for buying; in the other some features of the sale itself, mill location and a highly specialized product caused some employees to hold off. In the only other postwar sale where outsiders had an opportunity to buy (25 percent of a very small village) some employees had bought, or were buying, small farms nearby and moved to them at the time of the sale. Also, prices were high considering the houses though the location was good.

TERMS

Cash. All plans allow cash payment for houses and a good many sales include a few instances of such payments. One company which sold only a part of its village, and that gradually as occupants applied, allowed only a cash payment though some of its purchasers arranged credit in order to pay the mill. Prices announced were usually the cash figure, interest and amortization being taken care of in the schedule of payments. One mill allowed 5 percent, and another a flat $50 off for cash, and several had requests for such reductions.

Financing. With the single exception cited above every sale has had arrangements for installment paying. Even in the two villages that were sold, somewhat nominally, at auction the company carried the mortgage partly or entirely and even made payroll deductions for the payments.

In nearly all the prewar sales the mill carried the whole or some part of the mortgage; in a few a building and loan association had a first and the mill a second mortgage. One company arranged with the FHA to finance the purchases; however, the transactions were so involved and so slow, and the payment period (11 years) so long that the company changed over to the building and loan for the last half of the village. A company which sold to a real estate dealer for resale to its employees did so with the understanding that he give the regular building and loan period for payment. Another company which sold to outside parties for similar resale enlisted the cooperation of local banks and building and loan associations so that the purchasers could easily make their own arrangements. This plan had the advantage of flexibility for purchasers with varying amounts to pay in cash, and since the prices were low, none had difficulty in arranging mortgages. However, because of the price of the houses, the prospects for increasing business and full operation, the company stressed with the financing agencies the advantages of as rapid payment as possible, and a 5-year period was adopted.

The 5-year period in this prewar group of sales was the shortest in any plan. In three-fourths of the prewar sales the term was between 6 and 7 years, but six sales had a 10-year period, and five had all or part of their houses based on 10½ to 12-year payment periods. The odd lengths of time were the result of flat-rate payments such as the following:

Seventy-five cents a room a week.

1 percent of purchase price per month for 10 years.

1 percent of purchase price per month for 139 months.

$3.75 per week per $1,000 over a 7-year period.

$3.03 per week per $1,000 over a 10-year period.

In the 29 postwar sales covered by this study only three mills are carrying the mortgages and two others have a second mortgage, the building and loan having the first. All the others were financed through building and loan, bank, or investment company which in turn sold the paper to banks. Veterans who purchased often used G. I. financing. In two the term was 10 years, in all the other postwar sales the usual building and loan period, variously given as 6¼, 6⅔, or 6¾ years.

PAYMENTS

Down Payments. In about 10 percent of the sales no down payment was required. In prewar sales of this kind the mill was carrying all or part of the mortgage and there was no definite 30-day time limit. And yet the managers felt, as one said, it would be too hard on the people. In a few postwar sales the prices were so low that the local financing agencies considered the values sufficient to lend the total amount if the purchaser needed it.

The other 90 percent required a down payment when the contract for the house was signed. Most managers seemed to feel instinctively, and a few said, that it was better business and better psychology for the purchaser to thus clinch a bargain and to know from the beginning that he had some equity in the property. The only sale that "disappeared" was one where no down payment was required,[1] though that was probably not the only reason for its lack of success.

---

1. A specialized mill selling agent mentioned this sale as started by its company well before the war and, it was presumed, completed by the mill. The then president of the mill had died by the time of this study; the information clerk serving as intermediary between the writer and several officials of the company, brought back word that the mill had not sold its houses.

The usual down payment was 10 percent of the price. In one prewar sale 20 percent was required, but the mill paid better than average wages and there was no tight time limit. In the postwar period one financing agency required 20 percent and another 25 percent; in still another "the people paid what they could, ranging from $25 to $100," the mill lending them the balance not covered by the building and loan mortgage and taking a second mortgage.

The common practice when the mill carried the whole transaction was to give the purchaser the deed to the property when he had paid 10 percent. When other agencies financed, they followed their regular rule in this respect.

In prewar sales many purchasers, especially those with no prior warning and with a definite time limit on the sale, were unable to muster the 10 percent down payment. The financing arrangement had to include a way to make this possible. The system most used was pay roll deduction for six or ten weeks with rent continuing until the down payment was completed. Then rent ceased and the regular installments began. Several managers said with a touch of pride that their employees had the cash or sufficient credit in Morris Plan or regular banks to meet this payment.

In the postwar sales the vast majority of purchasers had the cash or easily obtained the credit outside for the down payment. A few mills offered assistance but the number needing it was too small for a systematic payroll deduction plan; the borrower just came in and paid by the month. In one case the problem was solved by having those few pay double installments for awhile; in another, down payments were waived in some hardship cases, in still another, the mill loaned the money to the few who needed it. In one quite sizeable sale the manager personally loaned or went on the notes of those who could not meet the down payment.

Method of Payment. In the prewar sales the most common practice was payment by weekly deduction from wages, even by some where the building and loan held a first mortgage. Some mills offered the purchasers their choice of deduction or payment at the office. Practically all chose deductions; for example, in a sale of 130 houses all except five chose deductions. This "vote" for deduction is an interesting commentary on the workers' attitude toward a mill practice which has been roundly damned for a generation. One company arranged for payments to be made at a bank although the mill owned the mortgages, and, of course, the two companies which sold 14 villages to outside parties for resale had no deductions; each buyer went to the office of the agency financing the purchase.

The picture is exactly reversed in the postwar sales. Only two have payroll deductions; three mills which are carrying the whole mortgage set up offices for collections, and in all the others payments are made in the office of the financing agency even though in some cases the mill holds a second mortgage. In two sales the people actually mail their payments to an outside financing agency.

This reversal of practice is due to several changes that have taken place since the prewar sales. Deductions for income tax and social security, for United States bonds, for the check-off in unionized plants, for the workers' share in an increasing number of mutually supported health, hospitalization, accident and group life insurance plans have multiplied the number of items taken from pay. Avoiding clerical work in the pay roll department and the bad psychological effect on the worker are excellent reasons, even if on the negative side. On the positive side several managers said they thought it was part of the new home owner's education to feel responsibility for making his payments.

For the same reason the payment of property taxes and insurance is different. Before the war most plans included these items in figuring the installments; since the war the majority of the purchasers pay directly to the county, town, and insurance company.

SIZE OF PAYMENT

The many ingenious ways of working out the length of the payment term were, like pricing the houses, a search for a basis which would yield weekly amounts the people could afford to pay. As far as could be determined within the limitations of this study, in no sale have the payments been more than the rents other employees were paying to private landlords in the vicinity; most have been less, and in a few cases only about half such rents.

The relationship to former mill rents, of course, depends on what those rates had been, length of payment term, and general price level of the houses. In the prewar sales where rent had been twenty-five cents a room a week and the purchase term between 6 and 7 years, the payments were roughly two to three times former mill rent. At rentals of fifty cents a room a week and the same 6 to 7-year term they were only 33 to 75 percent more. In a 12-year plan where rents had been fifty cents, payments were only about 15 percent more. In the 5-year plan with low prices and fifty-cent rents, they were about double former mill rent. Some typical payments are shown in Appendix II, pp. 126-27.

Irregular Payments. In a few of the earliest sales the mills ran into a period of short time, and some actually closed for awhile during the "recession" of 1937-38. All these were on payroll deduction plans and the company simply stopped deducting the payments. When full operation was resumed the people made up those deferred payments. At the few early sales which were financed outside, this problem did not happen to arise, but managements interviewed in early 1940 were sure there was little danger of purchasers being foreclosed. The low price of the houses, down payment, often a second mortgage by the mill, and a year or more of installments meant that a building and loan mortgage had been reduced sufficiently for safety, and several managers interviewed in 1940 said they would intervene for leniency in case of such an emergency. In the postwar sales the possibility for such conditions was not even mentioned in the face of full operation and high wages.

All plans, apparently those financed outside as well as by the company, allow for faster payment if the purchaser so wishes. Usually such extra payments must be in multiples of the regular amounts for simplification in bookkeeping. However, the writer was shown the payment records at several mills where all sorts of odd amounts were paid even by payroll deduction. Extra payments were usually counted as putting the purchaser ahead, but in a few plans they applied on the most distant payment. A manager where such a plan was used said the employees were puzzled and perhaps a bit suspicious, so that a little educational work was necessary to explain its advantages, namely, saving interest on the part of the debt bearing interest longest. They probably wanted to feel "ahead in case anything happened."

At nearly every sale some were paying faster than the schedule called for. In a 1936 sale on a 10-year basis one-fourth had finished paying when the writer visited the mill in 1940. In a 1939 sale, also on a 10-year basis, 33 percent had finished paying by 1947. In a 1938 6-year term sale, 80 percent paid faster, while in a 1945 6¾-year basis sale, 20 percent had paid out by 1947. A check of numerous collection records showed that from 10 to 25 percent were ahead. On the other hand, a number of managers said most of their people were content just to keep up with the regular payments even though good wages would seem to have made it wise to pay as fast as possible.

There have been two features of the sales that somewhat counterbalance the happy picture of eagerness to pay faster. Some purchasers have taken advantage of rising prices to refinance, thus getting a longer period to pay and sometimes some cash besides, or have negotiated loans with their paid-for or nearly paid-for houses as security. Others have yielded to the offers of high prices to sell their houses. Inasmuch as these and the few foreclosures concern the workers more than the selling process, they will be discussed in connection with the employees' problems.

In the vast majority of the sales the deeds include clauses limiting the use of the property to residential purposes. This restriction prohibits the building of stores, shops, garages and the like, with a few specifically mentioning amusement establishments and places for the sale of whiskey or "alcohol." It generally applies also to use of part of the existing house for business purposes. For example, in one case it was interpreted to forbid one room's being used as a beauty parlor. In cases where the villages were not very compact and had wedges or arms of privately owned property extending among the mill houses, little businesses, especially grocery stores, were already common, and the residential restriction was not included.

Almost all had a clause prohibiting sale to Negroes. In view of the recent Supreme Court decision this feature may be omitted in future sales, or remain in the form of a gentleman's agreement, or depend for enforcement only on public opinion.

There were probably many minor restrictions. It was impossible to cover every detail of such a complex situation with every busy mill executive interviewed. Some examples will illustrate the variety, and are in keeping with the characteristics of the mill village. A few specified only one house to a lot, a rule which may have to be modified; in one where this was a condition the lots are large enough to be divided. In several villages some of the new owners have already sold off a lot or built a house for a relative. One manager said the contract prohibited the "harboring of nuisances." The definition of a nuisance is capable of so many moral, physical, and subjective differences that enforcement of this restriction would seem to be difficult. Another stated—either quoting the contract or perhaps only euphemistically to the investigator—that there was to be no "objectionable house."

A few had an agreement that until the property was completely paid for there were to be no fundamental changes in the house without consultation with the company. The purpose was twofold. It protected the mill in case the purchaser should fail to keep up the payments and the house was thrown back on the company. As will be seen later, there has been practically none of this. Secondly, it could be used to dissuade a purchaser from undertaking too large and too expensive additions until he had paid for the house. One mill with such a clause has used it to discourage several buyers from covering their houses with brick or stone-patterned composition siding.

Although the information on this point is not too clear, a few mills apparently have clauses providing for repossession by the company under certain conditions even after it is fully paid for; at least they would give the mill first option to buy when a house is changing hands. Managers who had merely heard of such arrangements were more outspoken about them than those who had them. The former thought them unfair, impractical, and probably unenforceable: "If a mill wants to sell its houses it must really sell"; "They should not try to have their cake and eat it too"; "Such clauses would inevitably create a feeling of distrust and suspicion among the employees."

Many made the point that theirs was a bona fide sale with no strings attached. They said that the company was equally interested in getting rid of the houses and in seeing that as many employees as possible who wanted to should have the opportunity to become home owners. The elaborate arrangements for credit, the continuance of community services, assistance to the new home owners in their unaccustomed responsibilities bear out the honesty of their assertions.

CHAPTER 6

Some Post-Sale Problems

A COMPANY is not through with the village when it has set up policy, machinery, and personnel for the sale, nor even when the operation is over. The period of the sale is a busy one of adjustments, of explanation, of industrial relations with individuals and often with groups of employees. Other problems linger in the form of continuing relationships.

Several post-sale problems have so far been of minor importance because of general economic conditions. Only a few of the mills, those selling in the mid-1930's, have had to make good on the actual or implied promise to defer payments in case of short time or temporary shut-down. An occasional hardship case on account of protracted sickness or death of the chief wage earner was cited in many sales; these were taken care of in some simple, direct fashion which caused no complicating precedents because everyone understood the circumstances. In rare instances such a purchaser turned a house back to the mill which promptly sold it to another employee. Cases of this kind did not always reach the mill for adjustment because the family could sell at sufficient advance to pay off its indebtedness and have some cash besides. A good many managers mentioned resales which they knew to have grown out of such situations.

For the same reasons there have been practically no foreclosures, in a great majority of the sales not a single one. In a group of mills which has sold over 1,200 houses, there were just two foreclosures and these because of domestic difficulties in which neither husband nor wife wanted to continue paying on the houses.

The few mills which promised preferential treatment to purchasers in the matter of jobs were not put to much of a test because of labor shortages. Such provisions were made in some of the earlier sales, probably to overcome the uneasiness felt by the workers at this startling reversal of mill policy. Assurances of this kind were not mentioned as a feature of later sales.

In all the villages there has been some, and often a great deal of, swapping houses among the purchasers during the payment period. In the course of months or years they strike bargains with each other impossible to negotiate during the confused feeling at the time of the sale. When the company has anything to do with financing or payments all these exchanges naturally have to be cleared in its office, as do outright sales to non-employees. In the latter case the general practice is for the mill to be paid in full at the time of the transfer. However, some cases were encountered of non-employees coming in to make payments or being behind with payments. This sort of exception is natural in view of the direct, primary contacts and personal knowledge which a manager or superintendent has of the purchaser.

For sale plans which involve pay roll deductions there is, of course, a period of years during which many complications may arise. There are the payments faster than the schedule requires, a development expected and encouraged. There are occasional requests to omit deductions for special reasons, and someone must be given authority to pass upon such requests. More numerous are the cases where the person from whose wages the payments are deducted leaves the employ of the mill. If there are other members of the family on the pay roll they may arrange for deduction to be shifted; if not, some mills allow them to come in and pay just as those do which set up a separate collection office from the start. One large group of mills actually employed a collecting agent to make house to house calls for this purpose. These concessions make it possible for a family to change jobs without having to sell or refinance; a mill allowing this considers it worthwhile in general public relations and in having the good will of home owning workers who may presently return to its employ. However, a good many of these refinance their mortgages, securing the money to finish paying the mill when they leave its employ; indeed some mills require this. Several managers mentioned this group as contributing to the number who had "paid out." This problem will, of course, be of less concern in postwar sales since practically all pay at the office of the financing agent from the start.

A feature of continued relations in which the mills have differed widely is the amount and variety of aid to the purchasers in their new responsibilities. One company allowed the mill carpenters, plumbers, or painters to do all sorts of jobs, the employee-householder paying the mill for their time and for materials used. Several companies supplied materials and a good many furnished paint at cost, which, since these were bought by the mill at wholesale rates, meant a saving to the user. A company which sold shortly after the war agreed to continue its service of mowing lawns for the first summer. The manager feared that since lawn mowers had not yet come back on the market the well kept appearance of the community would suffer. Some arranged to have fire insurance carried on a group plan for lower rates. A few spoke of helping the whole group to have tax valuations kept at a figure somewhere near that at which the property had been listed under mill ownership, and so protect them from the inflated values of recent years.

Many a manager spoke of the calls on him or some other person in the company for advice on problems connected with their new responsibility. Some spoke a little proudly of these calls, feeling they reflected good relations and confidence, some a little wearily, and one said he asked them, "Now what would you do if the mill had never owned the house?" But then he went on and advised them. These calls drop off after a while as the people "get used to being homeowners."

A number of mills promised to make various miscellaneous additions, most of which were to bring all the houses up to the standard of the bulk of the village. Among these were instances of completing the job of putting in water connections, baths, or laying sidewalks. Several companies paid for water or electric meters if the change from flat rate payments to the mill had not already been made before the sale. Three companies finished paving streets in 14 villages.

CONTINUED SERVICES

One reason why disposing of the mill village posed so many problems is because the company usually carries on many services normally operated by a town government or public utility company. If the houses are inside the town limits some services may have already been performed by the town, but often not all. For the suburban village some services may already have been, or can easily be, tied in with town systems with or without extending corporate limits. Those completely away from incorporated towns have more difficult adjustments.

Of the villages covered by this study 49 are inside town limits; 43 inside those limits before the sale (in 4 of these a small part outside), 2 came in about the time of the sale and 2 afterwards. Of the 48 outside, 25 are close to corporate limits with continuous built-up areas connecting them with the town, so that some services are available and others may eventually be extended. Seven more were already entirely or partially connected with city water and sewer lines at the time of the sale. Three have started and two completed arrangements for sanitation districts to take care of street lights, water, and sewer. The remaining 10 are at present without good prospects of achieving these expensive improvements on account of small size, distance from another town, difficulties of terrain, or political rivalries which make annexation to the nearest incorporated town improbable in the near future.

Some of the actual solutions to these problems may be of interest.

Electricity. In over half the villages sold the householders were already paying a city or power system for current. In 25 more the change-over was made either at the time of the sale or a public system had agreed to take over at the time the manager was interviewed. Delays were sometimes experienced because of difficulties in securing meters, in which case the mill continued as prior to the sale. Seven companies were still providing current to 12 villages: one is on a low flat rate until house payments are over when it will go into the city system; in two a flat rate comparable to that of a nearby town is charged; in seven the mill buys wholesale, allows a minimum on a flat rate basis with the excess at rates lower than the regular price in the nearby system. The manager at one of these, a recent sale in Georgia, said he did not know how long he would be able to continue this, since he anticipated some legal difficulties because the company is not licensed as a public utility. The remaining company which still distributes current gives 5 kwh per room per month free as before the sale and charges at the rate of 5 cents a kwh for the excess. For those houses which have no employee, the mill charges for all the current used. The manager of this North Carolina company referred to no legal complication on this point since its sale in 1939.

Water. In 35 villages the householders were already paying a town or city system for water. In some 25 more they began to do so at the time of, or fairly soon after, the sale. In most of these cases the mill had been buying city water and distributing it to its tenants free with rent or at a small flat rate. One manager spoke of selling the water and sewer system to the city; another of "deeding" these and the streets to the city.

Of the dozen or so which still furnish water some charge a flat rate and some give it free. Three companies agreed to give water free until the house payments were completed; another "until some arrangements can be made," and still another until a nearby town takes it over. At one of the prewar sales both mill and houseowners face some difficulty when the now nearly completed payment is over. The nearby town prefers to sell water wholesale to the mill and justifiably so: the houses have only a spigot each so they are small customers; the piping was laid directly from house to house so that an expensive job of laying mains and connections will be necessary before meters can be installed. On the other hand, the mill, which incidentally has changed owners since the sale, has fulfilled the promise of free water for the payment period made by its predecessor, and the new management is eager to be rid of this obligation.

A few villages that have been sold get water from deep wells. The companies have been taking care of the pumps as before the sale. One small rural village visited by the writer depends for water on open wells with crank, rope and bucket.

Sewer. In the great majority of the villages all houses have inside toilets and about half of all houses sold have baths. Most of these are connected with city sewer systems, a few with the system built by the mill; some of the latter have already been turned over to the city or will be when payments are completed. In six villages part of the houses did not have inside toilets and sewer connections; in the four which were prewar sales mains have been run and nearly all the houses have inside toilets. The other two are similarly situated in or near the edges of towns and will eventually have mains available.

A dozen villages have outside toilets. Some of these are in the midst of setting up sanitation districts which will provide sewer facilities. At least half a dozen are poorly situated for such a solution: too small, too isolated or scattered over terrain which would make such a project too expensive. For even though the mill would be in the district and thus pay a large share of the taxes for amortizing the bonds, the cost to the individual home owner would still be large. A few of these have running water, and an occasional householder has installed a septic tank. Of those without inside toilets the mill is in most cases continuing to care for the outside toilets, though in two or three cases it was definitely stated that this was a responsibility of the owner. One mill man whose village has not been sold expressed the belief that those who do not continue such care may run afoul of the laws setting up standards as to type and cleaning of toilets in mill villages. But these are not mill villages any more; they are individually owned houses in unincorporated areas. It would seem that only such State laws or county health ordinances as relate to individual rural citizens would be applicable here.

Garbage and Rubbish. As is already clear many of the villages are in city limits where the houses have the regular garbage services of the town, either free with taxes or on a fee basis. Some of these near city limits get the services by paying a fee. One manager said the town refused to take over the third of the village not already inside corporate limits even on a fee basis and so the mill is continuing collection in that part for a year until an adjustment can be worked out. While this point was not covered as systematically in the interviews as most others, it appears that about a dozen collect garbage and rubbish as before the sale, even including a few which sold well before the war so that they have been continuing this service for a decade. In three, one old sale and two new, no one is collecting and the people burn or otherwise dispose of their waste materials as best they can. In one small village it looks as though leaves and other such trash are deposited in the single street running up a steep hill between the rows of houses. Indeed the casual observer can almost guess which villages have no systematic collection of rubbish. In these a heavy sprinkling of houses have trashy, cluttered yards.

Streets, Police, Fire Protection. The mills selling villages outside city limits seem to have been fairly successful in getting county or state road authorities to take over the care of the streets. Some continued to scrape dirt or gravel streets for awhile, and, as noted above, some have done additional paving since the sale.

Only a few mills that have sold had county deputies assigned to their areas to serve as police; these seem to have continued that arrangement with the sheriff's office. The majority are either within town limits or close enough for the jurisdiction of the town police to apply under State laws or local ordinances. Most suburban villages, therefore, have additional protection to that afforded by county constables.

Fire protection for those outside town limits is, naturally, somewhat scanty. Several managers said the fire fighting equipment of the mill has been used in the rare cases which arose.

Welfare and Community Work. Of the companies that have sold only 13 ever did very elaborate welfare or community work. Four of these had discontinued practically everything in their 20 villages well before the sale and disposed of their community houses, two before, one at the time of, and one after the sale. Four other companies with 13 villages had been doing somewhat less than in the heyday of welfare work; these continued their still fairly comprehensive programs. The other five companies with 14 villages continued about as much as they ever had, though, of course, the nature of the activities has undergone changes since the 1920's in keeping with interest and needs manifested by the people. Among those which had more modest programs during the 1920's a few had discontinued entirely, and some had decreased their work during the 1930's, though eight companies with 12 villages still did as much as ever. Some half dozen with a dozen villages had never done very much and have no program since the sale.

Mills which have no real community program help with athletic activities initiated by the workers just as they did before the sale. A good many managers, both with and without regular programs, said that the mill assists worthwhile community efforts which various autonomous groups start in the village. In ten villages where little is done by the mill the company retained one of the houses for a community center and meeting place for groups and clubs.

The range of community and welfare activities is now, as it always has been, very wide, from a little aid to a baseball team or a Boy Scout troop all the way to two companies with a staff of recreation and music leaders, club organizers and nurses, with a large community building, playground, and swimming pool. The purpose of the inquiry about this phase of the village was not to discover what is being done so much as to see what difference the sale has made. Apparently many mills reduced their expenditures for such things under the stress of finances during the depression or the feeling that the workers did not appreciate it during the tumultuous New Deal days. On the other hand, several managers were quite emphatic that they expect to do just as much community work as ever. One of these said he made a special point of announcing this policy at the time of the sale. He did not want the people to feel that the mill was cutting loose from all of the things they were accustomed to; he considered that the change to home ownership was innovation enough, that, if welfare work was worth doing before, it was more so now in order to hold the employees.

CHAPTER 7

Response to a Sale

THERE are as many complicating factors for the employee-purchasers as for the company-sellers. These begin at the announcement of a sale and continue through the period of adjustment to home ownership and community responsibility.

THE FIRST REACTION

The first reaction is that of shock. And no wonder! There has long been something immutable about the mill village. Some employees had in the past tried to buy a house or a lot from the company and "they wouldn't sell a foot." A mill house is not like one rented from an ordinary landlord who may decide to occupy or sell or give it to his son. It is part of the equipment for carrying on a job, and the relationship of landlord-tenant is subsidiary to that of employer-employee. For two or three generations the next question after inquiring for a job has been: "What about a house?" If in recent years the reply was more often than not that the mill had no house available, this was actually or subconsciously accounted for by the fact that the mill was operating two, and later three shifts. In these years more and more of those who had sufficient urge for ownership had sorted themselves out and bought homes with or without company aid, with many mills assisting in one way or another. Others who preferred not to live on "the mill hill" or were not lucky enough to secure a mill house had made an adjustment to private rental. Therefore, the company tenants have to a large extent become a concentrated group who do not want to own or feel that they cannot do so. To them housing by the mill is a part of their psychology and economy. At one of the earliest sales the people simply did not believe the mill would sell. They did not come in to make further inquiries or sign up to buy. The matter languished for a while and the company, under its plan of preference to occupants, other employees, and finally non-employees, sold one house to an outsider. The workers saw the company really meant business about this strange new policy and began to buy briskly.

In a few cases the sales were approached in such a way as to soften the impact. Some of these have already been suggested and will be discussed more fully in a later chapter. However, in fully three-fourths of the sales covered by this study there were various degrees of shock. Workers said, "It was just like a bombshell"; "This village has never been in such a commotion"; "Everybody asked, 'what shall we do?'" Social workers and others who had close contact with the people testified to this sense of shock. The writer visited prewar and postwar sales soon after the announcement and heard many evidences of this feeling in personal interviews with workers. Some managers admitted that "the people were right much surprised"; some who claimed they were not were contradicted by other witnesses.

In general it can be said that the first sales in a given area are apt to cause most shock. Subsequent announcements may cause surprise but not quite dismay. The people will have heard something of how sales operate and some have friends and relatives who have bought houses in village sales. And yet in one prewar and one postwar case earlier sales in the close neighborhood did not seem to soften the blow. In one of these the person describing the feeling was asked why the people could have been so surprised when the company had sold villages at other plants. "Well, it's like death or an automobile accident—it can happen to the other fellow but not to you. We just *knew* the company wouldn't sell this village." A manager who sold a dozen villages in quick succession claimed that only those in the first had any shock; the rest, he added grimly, "saw the handwriting on the wall."

And so when the announcement is made, "the people talk of nothing else," each contributing some new rumor, uncertainty, or disadvantage. Some are suspicious and think there is a trick in it, there must be for the mill to sell its houses; that the mill will sell the house but not the lot, that it will retain a strip of land along the front of the lot, that it cannot or will not give a good title to the property, that it will "fix some way to get the houses back." Some think the sale is to tie them to the mill and make it easier to lay off workers in dull times. Some say home owners will be laid off first because they will have to stay, while others claim those who buy will be rewarded by job preference. A rumor spreads that the mill is going to close up and this is a first step. In some situations it is to keep out the union, in others it is to weaken the union they have.

They do not know the exact prices of their houses and the management's statement that these will be fair, or reasonable, or generous may turn out to be very different from their ideas on the subject. A stubborn few say, "If the mill expects us to buy, it will have to fix some way for us to pay," but the announcement's phrases about liberal terms and installment payment are not reassuring to a family with little cash and no credit.

One mill collected 18 different rumors, suspicions, and misunderstandings about a sale in its neighborhood. Profiting by this knowledge, it was able to forestall and scotch quickly most such that rose in its own sale some months later.

The feeling of confusion at the announcement is mingled with the helpless feeling of compulsion to buy. Most mill managers interviewed in 1940 said proudly or defensively that they put no pressure on the employees to buy; that the latter were appreciative of the opportunity and conscious of the bargain they were getting as was shown by the fact that they signed up promptly. But most of them also said—though not in just this juxtaposition—that houses for sale in the vicinity were scarce and high priced, while those for rent were scarcer and rents were higher than the payments on the purchase plan. As many workers said to the writer, "You are forced to buy; otherwise you have to look for a job somewhere else, for there are no houses around here." In the postwar sales with the housing shortage far greater, managers did not bother to protest the compulsion to buy. Even more than before the war the people stand in line to sign up lest employees not already in company houses buy from under them.

This feeling of pressure is increased by the fact that they have only a short period, 30 days in most sales, to decide; a month to make up their minds to do what some have assumed would never be necessary, desirable, or possible for them. The village system has accustomed the southern textile worker to moving as a way of escaping living or working conditions he may not like, to find a job if his mill runs irregularly, as a change if only from one monotony to another, and as one man, who had moved six times in a radius of 30 miles, said, "a way to see something of the world." It has educated him in considerable skill in the process. Should one buy at this particular mill with its policies, its operational history, its type of product? A worker who had shortly before refused to buy the village house he occupied said with fierce disgust, "Did you ever hear of this kind of mill running 6⅔ years?" Should one buy in this particular area with few or no mills within 15 to 30 miles?

The feeling of disquiet is further increased by the fact that a family has to take the house in which it happens to be. As has been pointed out, there is always some moving within the village, families edging closer to the more desirable center, moving to larger houses as the children grow up, to smaller as they leave home. Even the family that stays in the same house for years may not like it, or its location or the neighbors, but they put up with it because they feel, as any tenant does, that it is temporary. One old lady complained for 25 years for lack of a small improvement that would have cost her only a few dollars, but she did not make it because she might not stay there long enough to get the benefit and she was "not going to fix up the house for the mill." All of a sudden, you are "stuck with it."

Theoretically there can be any amount of changing about and most sale plans allow swapping of options before purchase. Practically it does not work out very well except for a few direct swaps because the difficulties mount in geometric ratio to the number involved. The exchanges made after the sale is over and at some stage in the payment period far outnumber the swapping during the sale itself.

"They've got it fixed so you have to buy" the house you are in and quickly. The occupant knows that non-housed employees or outsiders are ready to snap up the house; one man "heard" that 17 other employees had applied for the house he was in if he did not take it. Nobody can afford to be left out in the game of pussy-wants-a-corner. A selling agent told of a man who firmly refused to buy when his village was sold. A month or two later at the sale of another village by the company he showed up grinning to buy the house he occupied in that village. After thinking things over he had decided it was a good thing to buy but his chance in the first village was gone; he moved the 30-odd miles to the other mill, got a job and a house and was ready when the sale started. At that, he was luckier than most would be, for few mills have a house so promptly for a new or even a transferred employee.

When the occupant hears the price of his house it usually sounds like a big sum of money. To be sure many of the people have bargained to pay, in installments, amounts half as large for a used car and quite as large for a new one. But that was something they chose to buy, something that would aid rather than limit mobility. This investigator happened to visit a number of villages very soon after the sale had been announced and encountered many of the first reactions to prices. In prewar sales some said indignantly, "They want $800 for this old house"; "These old houses did not cost more than $500 or $600 to build 30 years ago and now they ask us to pay $800 or $900 for them." Well, of course, there is the matter of the lot and such improvements as streets, lighting system and, in many cases, water and sewer lines. But it must be remembered that the people were not accustomed to property taxes and assessments for improvements. Some said, "I've been paying rent on that house for 20 years. If I can buy it now in 10 years with payments not much more than rent, I have already paid for it." This argument ignores the economic fact that the rents were only about half enough to keep the house in repair. It also ignores the legal fact that unless there has been an agreement for part of the payment to count as amortization the rent would go on indefinitely. All these reactions simply reflect the confusion of tenant psychology suddenly confronted with the problem of home owning.

In the postwar sales there seems to have been less shock at prices two and three times as high as those before the war. In the interim the people became used to wages of $40 and $50 a week and more with frequent overtime. More of their fellow workers have been paying high private rentals or buying houses at prices greater than they are asked to pay. One woman said she had recently "bought my house for twenty hundred dollars. That wasn't so much, was it?" As sales have become more common there are signs that the people are growing resigned to the idea. A woman who had recently bought a mill house said, "We didn't want to buy but we had lived here 20 years and didn't want to move. Besides, if we had gone to another mill it might up and sell and we might not like there as well as we do here."

Another factor that helped in the adjustment to the prices was getting other people's evaluations. In every village someone would have an offer to take the house off his hands at a profit. An occasional skeptic would have a real estate dealer set a price or inquire at some financial agency as to what size loan it would make on the property. The results would circulate as rapidly as rumors about the sale itself.

As the buyers learn more about the terms the whole proposition begins to look a little better. They learn that the company will give credit or has arranged with local agencies to give it. They learn what the weekly or monthly installment will be and see that they can manage it. The period of adjustment has begun.

The sale of a village has some immediate effects on the way of life of the purchasers. In the prewar sales the first effect was on their buying habits. In that period the people rarely had the cash for the down payment and so had to make it over a period of two or three months either with rent continuing or regular payments beginning. The two payments took a sizeable part of their weekly earnings.

This actual tightening of their budgets, together with their feeling of unease at the new venture, caused them to cut down sharply on the buying of certain kinds of commodities. Nearby filling stations almost uniformly reported far less gas sold for awhile. In one town a grocer remarked that the sale of "fancy goods" stopped abruptly and the people bought only the simplest staple foods.

Installment sellers found their markets suddenly, if temporarily, gone. In a town where the sale of many surrounding villages went on in quick succession they had difficulty collecting on goods already sold and other merchants found sales curtailed. For a while at least this group could not share very heartily in the general community's cliché about the contribution of home ownership to the making of a good town. Even the welfare agencies felt the repercussions in increased requests for aid to aged and infirm dependents. In other towns merchants admitted that they expected sales would be off, but held to the philosophy that in the long run business would be better.

In the postwar sales this first reaction was far less noticeable. A large proportion had the cash for the down payment, so there were few making double payments. And while regular installments on the principal outstanding were some two to four times former rent, their wages were sufficient to meet them without changes in buying habits conspicuous enough for general remark.

THE NEW HOME OWNERS

Another result follows close on the heels of a sale. The purchasers immediately feel the release from the renter-transient psychology. Many a family had lived for years in a house, but they always "might move." Now they would be there. They began to care for and improve their houses and lots. Every mill official interviewed except one bore witness to this fact. The one exception had noticed no general activity due, he thought, to the fact that the houses were in good condition and the company had long laid stress on appearance and planting around the houses. But even in this case the head of the local union said the people had begun to "fix up."

Everybody testified to this result: not only mill managers, union officials, and workers themselves but school principals and teachers, welfare, community service and social workers of all kinds, neighboring shop and filling station keepers, newspaper men, literally all whose work or situation put the village under their observation. All said that the majority of purchasers began to show evidences of a feeling of permanency and an owner's interest and pride. They plant grass, flowers, and shrubs. They prune trees and smooth off unlevel lots, and at the older sales have sometimes built retaining walls. Some mills have systematically planted shrubs and ornamental trees around the houses only to see them neglected and misused or destroyed by many of the tenants. There was only a little irony mixed with the managers' pleasure in reporting that after the sale most of the people began to take care of them and replace those destroyed. Social workers whose territories included several villages said you could tell immediately one that had been sold by the activity going on in the yard, in a few months by the shrubbery and flowers, while those that had been sold two or three years were distinguishable to the most casual passer-by on account of planting and generally "lived in" appearance.

Some paint their houses soon after purchasing even if this is not particularly necessary, using a different color from the neighbors and often putting a trimming in bright contrasting color. This is obviously an effort to make them different; some add blinds or change the position of the steps, partly, no doubt, for the same reason. Some cover the house with white asbestos shingles which are mildly decorative as well as protective. Since the war a few in practically every village visited, new and old sales alike, have covered their houses with asphalt or tar composition sheeting to imitate brick or stone. While the result is questionable on aesthetic grounds, it saves painting, makes the house warmer and certainly makes it different.

A few of the many revealing instances can be cited to show the quickness of the response. One company which had a standing offer of rooted cuttings and slips from shrubbery around the mill had for years received only an occasional request; right after the sale it was deluged with calls. In a prewar sale the writer called on a young couple who had signed up for the purchase of their home three days before. They had lived in the house for two or three years, but that Saturday afternoon the young man was busy making screens for the windows. They had a parlor with the inevitable overstuffed suite, a thick rug, cabinet radio, a kitchen with a gleaming big mechanical refrigerator and bright new linoleum, but until the house was really to be theirs they had not been willing to spend the relatively small amount for the comfort of screens. A similar incident was related by a mill owner who sold his houses gradually, carrying on the separate deals himself. After the signing of the papers for one house he went on up the street on the same errand to another employee. Returning an hour later he saw the first man arriving home with a roll of screen wire. One woman had been inconvenienced for years by having to move all of her glass jars of home canned fruit and vegetables out of an unceiled pantry every cold spell—"the mill wouldn't ceil it for me." Her pleasure in the fact that her husband had ceiled it as soon as they had signed up for the house was unalloyed by the retrospection that he could have done it years before with very little expense and work.

Many incidents reflect the habit of dependence on old disciplinary powers of the employer-landlord. Managers, or more often super-intendents, at first had requests to make a neighbor get rid of chickens or dogs or keep them penned. They had complaints of a noisy household or of trespassing children, especially if they were de-structive of the now more cherished grass and shrubbery. These people were nonplussed when reminded that the mill no longer had any authority over the houses.

Many changes reflect the relief from village rules and regulations. In one or two villages that had rules against keeping dogs, many families immediately got dogs. Many managements discourage the building of fences, and apparently most forbid their being built in front of the house. Hardly a village that has been sold is without a sprinkling of fenced-in front yards, some neat pickets, some less good looking wire and a few which actually detract from the looks of the place. But they satisfy the owners' need to keep in a child or to keep out intruders, to show where the lines of his property run, to make his place look different, or just to do something he had not been allowed to do before.

Few mills allow tenants to put up unsightly outbuildings, and still fewer tenants will build good substantial structures which they may move off and leave. After a sale some put up neat, painted garages; more put up make-shift sheds which, like a number of the fences, do not improve the appearance.

Few, if any, mills allow a tenant to operate a store in his house or to build a store on the lot, even if some rare tenant would be willing to build on mill-owned land. One man, as soon as he got his deed, set up a store in a room of his house. In the villages where there was no provision for restriction to residential use, little stores have sprung up all over the place.

During the sale of his village a mill official saw a quite elderly woman hacking away at a good sized umbrella tree in her front yard. He stopped to chat, remarking that the job looked a little unhandy for her—why didn't she let her husband or son do it? "I couldn't wait," she replied, "I've hated this Chiney berry tree the whole time

I've lived in this house, but it belonged to the company and they wouldn't cut it down. Yesterday we signed up to buy the house and I 'lowed I'd get rid of it."

The pride in owning is quickly expressed in standing up for one's rights. A number of instances were cited where the purchasers stopped the use of little paths across their lots. Often these short cuts had been used for years with no objection by the tenant on the grounds of nuisance, lack of privacy, or their right as tenants of the property. As soon as they signed up they stopped the trespassing with a complaint or with a fence. In one case the garbage truck driver was in the habit of turning a corner too closely, nipping off a little at the angle of the lot. Soon after the sale the purchaser went to the mill office to demand that the truck be kept off his property, threatening to sue the company if it was not. The mill representative gravely assured him that this would be done, and when the somewhat truculent owner was gone, exclaimed to his associates, "Thank God they've got that much spunk!" The company was continuing the garbage collection entirely free.

The type of improvement that is started first depends on what the purchasers have bought. In a few excellent and well maintained villages the people began putting up Venetian blinds and replacing oilcloth in kitchen and bathroom with linoleum. Where the sidewalks as well as the streets were paved they began to lay brick or concrete walks from the steps; in some villages which had walks to the houses they began building brick or concrete steps. Where the houses had not been underpinned they began putting curtain walls between the pillars; in one village sold only a few months before the visit by the writer, many had already underpinned and most of the others had a pile of brick ready for the operation.

In villages where the houses have sewer connections but no bath some soon add a bath. In those that have only running water at least a few soon added both bath and toilet although they have to provide septic tanks. At several villages reference was made to the fact that some had had, or were waiting for, the installation of heavier wiring so they could have electric stoves.

In villages that were sold as they stood, without general overhauling, purchasers began at once to make repairs. These ranged all the way from mending steps to new roofs; from small jobs that could be done by members of the family to arranging F.H.A. loans for fundamental repairs. There have not been many sales without either general repair or fairly good routine maintenance. Consequently not many villages need immediate and expensive renovations. This is fortunate, since the payments on the loans added to those on the house itself might prove difficult under ordinary circumstances and impossible if wages should decline or work become irregular.

In nearly every village a few purchasers began quickly to make fairly important changes in the house. Naturally, most of these have occurred in the prewar sales, some adding a room or even a story to the house. The war shortages of materials served to hold down major building operations. This was no doubt just as well, or some would have overreached themselves. However, the prewar purchasers who bargained for heavy expenditure had the advantage of small payments on house and improvements out of sharply increasing wages. Postwar purchasers are not so favorably situated. Repairs and small improvements went on all during the war since one was occasionally able to pick up a little material and most could do the work themselves. The men are handy with tools and are frequently tinkering with repairs which they would previously have called on the mill to make, or which would have been neglected until a general village repair. Innumerable incidents of this kind were cited.

Making the home more sightly and more comfortable extends to the inside. Most mills, even when hard pressed financially, paint the outside of the houses frequently enough for protection; few paint the inside as often, and fewer still do so often enough to please the good housekeeper or overcome the ravages of the poor one. Occasionally the mill will furnish the paint for an inside job if the tenant will apply it. The managers of two such remarked ironically that far more now buy the paint as well as apply it. Some purchasers of ceiled houses put up beaverboard both for warmth and a better surface. In a village where the houses had high ceilings some of the new owners put in new low ceilings to make the rooms easier to heat. A few have put in central heating.

When the purchasers have adjusted their thinking to ownership and their budgets to the payments, they are in the market for more and better furniture. This was especially true in the prewar sales in the face of increasing regular work and rising wages. Installment sellers, strangled for a few months, began to have a field day. In one such town where a good many villages were sold, a local social worker feared that they were exploiting the families by pressing the new pride in their homes too hard and loading them up with furniture beyond their needs and ability to pay. An adult education director in the same town had many requests for classes in "interior decoration"—simple courses in color and arrangement and the purchasing of furnishings.

As it turned out, these, like the early buyers who made substantial improvements, had no difficulty in meeting their payments, and have probably congratulated themselves that they bought when they did. Again those in postwar sales run a greater risk.

Many mill managers spoke of this tendency to buy more and better furnishings and equipment since the purchase of the house. Several, especially those in small companies who knew the families well, cited houses that were "furnished as well and comfortably as anybody's house." The same expression was used by workers describing homes, one or two pridefully adding the significant remark that such and such a home "looked inside like any Mrs. Rich's house." It is clear that all these witnesses had in mind rather highly selected cases. A visiting teacher in a town where many mill houses were sold a decade ago gives a better cross section. In her 30 years service there she has known the people intimately and been in and out of their houses. She said that the better wages in recent years have meant great improvement in the furnishings of mill workers' homes over the bare, dreary rooms she used to see years ago. Her contact throughout the whole process has convinced her that their ownership has stimulated much of this practically universal interest in putting part of the increased earnings into furnishings. What they have bought is sometimes showy, and not always in too good taste, but it is usually comfortable and vastly satisfying to the owners. She added, wryly, that not all had brought their standards of housekeeping up to the level of their new possessions.

This feeling of ownership manifests itself as soon as they "sign up" for the house, reflecting perhaps their experience with installment buying. But they have a special eagerness to get the deed and have it recorded at the county seat. Finishing the down payments, getting the deed and the final payment are all stages in the process in which they take pride and pleasure. Getting the deed represents release from the landlord-boss psychology. In the prewar sales when jobs were not always to be had for the asking it took a special form. A number of instances were cited where a man flourished his deed before his "super" and said with a smile, "Well, you can fire me but you can't make me move." Some felt this release even when signing up for the house, and phrases about firing vs. moving were common coin in the half serious exchange of pleasantries accompanying that little ceremony. The writer heard it from many workers in 1940.

The change in the job situation modified this expression. In 1947-48, one heard more commonly, "Now I can work anywhere I want to without having to move."

One observer had several widely scattered purchasers point up their satisfaction in their status as property owners by saying that they were the first in their family in two, three, as many generations as they knew, who had ever owned a foot of land. A man on the street of a village—incidentally where the announcement of a sale about a year earlier had produced considerable shock—was asked how the people liked the idea of buying their homes. He grinned and declared it was the "finest thing ever struck this town. Why, there are people here who didn't know what it was to own," pausing to think of an adequate measure, "an extra pair of shoes. Now they have their homes and before long will have them paid for." He pridefully pointed out his own home nearby.

The associates of a mill president unaccountably could not locate him for hours. When he finally showed up he said he had spent the afternoon "on old man Tom Blank's porch rocking and reminiscing." This employee had sent a note saying he had made his last payment, adding, "When I came to work here 20 years ago I was in debt. You fixed it so I could own my home. It's mine now and I want you to come and see it." The president had obliged.

Every sale produces its share of human interest incidents like those which this investigator stumbled upon. Every sale has been followed by improvement and at least good care by the majority of the new owners. At every sale which took place long enough ago to make the observation significant the managers said the new owners had done well—unexpectedly well—on upkeep. Practically all said they had done as well as the mill would have done, and a few said they had done better. An editor in a town where many mill owned houses were sold well before the war said the appearance of the whole town had profited by the improvement in sections that had long been dreary and dull. A county school official speaking of the same areas advanced the opinion that the new home owners had been stimulated to improve their houses and grounds by the neat new cottages of their fellow workers who had built on the highways radiating from that busy industrial town. This represented such an amazing reversal of the usual flow of influence that it would have been discarded as captious from one less qualified by long and close contact.

The buyers of double houses have, by all available data, proved to be satisfactory landlords. However, this factor has not been thoroughly tested because of the relatively few double houses sold and for lack of time: 8 of the 12 villages with such houses are among post-war sales. A few have vacated the other side of the house to make room for a relative, most often a returning G.I. son. Most have rented to the family occupying at the time of the sale. They have charged reasonable rents, more than the old mill rate before the sale but less than private rents in the vicinity. Even so, this was frequently enough to carry the payments on the whole house. One man was cited who charged exactly half the payments because he thought that was fair. He will probably revise his thinking when he has to make extensive repairs.

THE OTHER SIDE OF THE PICTURE

The enthusiastic and often glowing statements about interest, improvement and upkeep are nearly always applied to "the majority," to "90 percent," even to "98 percent." Naturally not every family feels this pride and interest. Nearly every village sold some years ago has a few places which stand out like the proverbial sore thumb. For every mill manager who can see from the mill office window several houses with great improvement there is one, and often the same one, who can also see a house or two that has had nothing done to it since the sale. In several cases a house unpainted for years, with steps rotting and yard cluttered was in full view of the office. Critics who have long accused the mills of maintaining this area above the level of the village as a whole for window dressing purposes will no doubt get a certain sardonic satisfaction out of that kind of situation.

Differences in upkeep and appearance are due to differences in people; they are the inevitable result of the rule to sell to the occupant and the well-nigh necessity for him to buy. For not every family that happens to be in a mill house at any given time is potentially a prideful home owner. In a few places, the management, having a sale in mind for a long time, has been gradually weeding out undesirables. But a man may be an excellent employee and a desirable citizen and yet not keep a tidy place. Besides it is impossible to be certain beforehand how ownership psychology will affect particular people. This fact was pointed up by the observation of a young businessman who took over for the mill much of the detail succeeding the sale itself. When he first heard the mill might sell he thought of the constant and expensive care the company had given to the houses and offered strong if gratuitous advice to the manager against the sale: the people wouldn't keep the houses up nor their yards clean; the village would run down, become undesirable and get a bad name; property values would go down and even those who kept up their houses would be disgruntled. Six years after the sale he said he had been wrong on all counts. But his greatest surprise had been in the response of individual families. Some who formerly gave maintenance crews constant trouble had done most to their houses and had among the best looking places in the town; others who had been good-to-excellent tenants under mill care now had untidy premises and houses neglected even in such essentials as paint and roofs.

To the observer familiar with mill villages this occasional run-down or unkempt place stands out prominently. Under mill maintenance all houses are usually painted at once, so that all are fresh or medium or beginning to need a coat for protective purposes. Under mill maintenance tenants cooperate willingly, under persuasion or under pressure on the collection of rubbish and trash for removal. Where this service has been discontinued many of the backyards are cluttered; even where it has been continued by the mill or taken over by the town, there is an occasional such yard in almost every village. The favorite pieces of rubbish are old automobiles in various stages of disintegration.

The writer made a point of driving about the villages that had been sold. In those where there had been time for the development of differences, a very rough tally seemed to show that about 1 in 10 was noticeably below average in appearance and 1 in 15 or 20 strikingly so.

RESALES

On this negative side of the picture there are, in addition, some who show the ultimate in lack of interest in home owning—or the inability to resist a good profit—by reselling. And indeed not all reselling is necessarily on the negative side. In transactions involving thousands of families, changes in their own and outside situations make some selling inevitable and even desirable.

Not all managers had exact data on the number, to say nothing of the wisdom of the resales. But enough knew the approximate number of resales to show that the situation is very mixed. The reason for the differences is by no means clear. Two companies whose sales of six villages in 1938-39 totaled nearly 1200 houses reported that 50 percent of the houses have changed hands. All these villages were in cities with other textile and varied employment, and yet the purchasers had been chiefly other employees of the company. On the other hand, the managers of three companies which sold before the war 30 villages made up of nearly 3500 houses said the proportion of resales had been very small. Their estimate was corroborated by school principals, community and social workers who are in close touch with the families. Some of these villages are near many mills, while others were convenient only to those of the company which sold the houses.

Likewise in two small prewar sales of less than 50 houses each, the manager of one said 75 percent had changed hands, while the other said none had been resold. In both cases the mill was getting workers from nearly every former mill house. In a village of about 100 houses sold in 1939 only 15 percent had been resold. In another village in the same town and of about the same size sold in 1938, between 70 and 80 percent had been resold and some several times, though 60 percent were currently owned by employees. Here the difference may lie in the fact that the latter village had somewhat more substantial houses, that it had paved streets and sidewalks and was closer to the center of town. The prices offered would consequently be more tempting. A manager who had sold 170 houses in 1939 said 25 percent had changed hands, adding in an injured tone that not one offered his house to the mill, though everyone knew the company was in great need of places for new key men to live. Some others who had fairly accurate resale figures were as follows:

20 out of 190 sold in 1939, of which 13 had been bought by one man for rental purposes. He charges "reasonable rents and favors employees of the company."

2 out of 70 sold in 1941, one because the family needed a larger house.

12 out of 100 sold gradually from 1940 to 1945, chiefly to other employees.

10 out of 71 sold in 1940, all except two resold to other employees.

25 out of 200 sold in 1939, mostly to non-textile people.

57 out of 87 sold in 1940, mostly to non-employees.

In these prewar sales the common comment, with many illustrations of actual prices, was that the purchasers resold at double the mill price if the transaction took place a few years ago, and rising to three and four times in recent deals.

At the postwar sales there has not been time for quite so much reselling. The higher price level makes the offers somewhat less tempting. Profits cited ranged from $200 or $300 to $1,000, with only an occasional case of double the mill figure. No matter how recent the sale at least one or a few have resold. The highest estimate was

10 percent out of a sale of some 250 houses that had taken place less than a year earlier.

Nearly everybody interviewed who had close touch with the village was able to cite instances of purchasers who had sold and regretted it: had to live with relatives, bought a house that was poorer or on a road impassable in bad weather, was paying high rent, sometimes for that very house. The predicament of such a seller was sometimes said to have dampened the enthusiasm of his neighbors toward selling; the writer talked to workers who told, with regret in their voices, of refusing "mighty good offers." Another danger cited was the assiduous offers of loan agents to remortgage houses paid for or nearly paid for, with all the possibilities of foreclosure if "times get bad." So far conditions have prevented these from coming to a head and exercising a restraining influence on others.

All these informants were either clearly or admittedly talking about striking individual cases, except for the few villages where a high percentage of resales was reported. They said at once or in some other connection that in the main the people were holding on to their property.

The sale of a mill village changes the way of life for the people. They must make decisions which they had very likely never thought would be necessary. They have new responsibilities and, in times of rising values, new temptations. On the whole the new home owners have resisted the temptation to quick profit, have measured up to the responsibilities of maintenance, and have shown their pride by improvements. Their response to so unaccustomed and unpleasant a subject as property taxes is perhaps a sort of index. In two counties where a great many mill houses have been sold information was sought as to their standing in this respect. In one the tax official was interested enough to make a quick count: there were relatively fewer owners of former mill houses on the delinquent list than of other property holders. In the early days of sales many had come in to pay taxes and had to be reassured that the mills were still paying them, this item having been included in setting up the payment scheme. In the other county the tax official was indignant at a question as to their relative standing in this respect: "Of course they pay their taxes. They are just as responsible citizens as anybody else."

CHAPTER 8

The Union and Village Sales

AMONG the many changes affecting the mill village institution during the last decade none represents so great a departure from traditional ways as the right to organize. Spasmodic efforts at union-ism in southern textile mills failed for forty years. While many other factors contributed to the failures, the really fundamental obstacle was the company village with housing available for practically all workers. The mill, like most other employers in the country, could fire a worker who tried to organize a union. But the mill, by the act of discharging, automatically removed him from the community, since he had to give up his house when he lost his job. The risks to such a worker, on the one hand, and the removal of potential leader-ship, on the other, kept unions from growing up from within. The village is private property—the houses, the meeting places, and the streets—and so an "outside agitator" was a trespasser who could be removed by a warning or by actual arrest. Therefore outside stimu-lation to unionism was difficult and uncertain.

The National Recovery Act of 1933 came at a crucial moment for southern mill workers. During the late 1920's the ever-spreading "stretch-out" had created a sense of grievance; during the early 1930's low wages and short time had added a feeling of helplessness. Sud-denly the new law shortened hours, raised wages, and gave protection in the right to organize. The electrifying change produced the great textile strike of 1934. The union's success in closing mills scattered all over the South warned the employers of the potentialities of or-ganization; its failure to hold its recruits and carry on its program showed the leaders that they must build more slowly and solidly.

This they have done, although, even after more than a decade, the union claims only some 20 to 25 percent of the southern textile workers as members. It found that the workers needed convincing as well as training and experience in unionism, and that the old controls, though weakened, were not entirely gone. But the influence of the union is stronger than the figures on membership and contracts indicate. This was proved by wage raises in recent years: when unions won an increase, non-union mills hastened to grant similar raises, and on several occasions led off in the procession. The union probably was not strong enough to stop village sales even if its general policy of opposition to them had been more clear-cut than it was.

The presence of the union in the industry and the threat of more unionism, together with the dulling of the old tools for fighting it, were part of the background out of which grew the move to sell the villages. Any further correlation between sales and the presence of unions is not evident from the status of unionism at the points of sale. Of the 97 villages covered by this study, 19 were sold by mills which had contracts with unions at the time of the sale. The villages were owned by 12 companies. In five more, sold by two firms, contracts were agreed upon after the sale; among the employees of one the union was active at the time though a contract was not signed until three years afterwards; in the other there was little union activity until well afterwards. In seven other sales by four concerns union activity ranged from moderate to very brisk; in all but one village it died out before achieving a contract. Thus in 31 villages owned by 18 companies sales took place when there was a union strong enough to have registered a definite reaction. At a number of other sales some organizational work was going on at the time but, from all information available, had not reached a stage where the union attitude would have been influential with employers or workers.

The situation, however, is even more mixed than this summary shows. The action of firms controlling several plants will illustrate this fact. One sold, years ago, the villages in a locality where the union was growing vigorously but not those at its plants 100 miles away where organizing efforts were active in the vicinity and had won contracts in neighboring mills. A second sold the village at a unionized plant and followed it immediately with a sale at another located in an area which probably had as little organizational activity as any in the textile South. A third company sold all its villages, those at plants under contract and those where unions had not, nor since have, had much response. A completely unionized company sold the village at a closed-down plant and is building houses at an operating unit a mile or so away. Two companies sold parts of their large villages as an experiment: one was completely unionized, the other not at all. Still another company sold the villages of its closely grouped mills years ago when unionism was discredited among the workers in the area because of their then recent unhappy experience; another sold widely scattered villages in only one of which there had been efforts at organization and these had not, nor have yet, reached the stage of an election.

The situation is just as contradictory among companies which have sold no villages. Companies from Virginia to Alabama that have had contracts with the union for years have not sold. Neither have hundreds without unions sold; one of the largest in the South is adding extensively to its villages. A company which the unions have repeatedly and unsuccessfully tried to organize has not sold; an inquiry on this point to a casually encountered employee elicited as startled a negative as it would have a quarter of a century ago: "Selling the mill houses! Goodness, no! The company is buying all the land it can." This worker knew about sales since several had taken place within 20 miles.

In a few cases (which will be noted presently) unionization or the threat of it may have been a definite factor in the decision to sell. On the other hand there is no way of knowing how many refrained from selling lest the move cause dissatisfaction and increase interest in joining a union.

EARLY UNION POLICY

The first dozen sales, from 1934 to 1938, were of villages where there was no union and little organization activity. Between 1938 and 1940 the nearly 40 villages sold included 2 where the union had a contract and 8 where, although the union lacked a contract, it was active and influential. Thus up to 1940 the direct experience of union leaders with sales was limited. Their attitude on the subject was based both on general principles and on the current economic situation.

In the main the attitude of union leaders interviewed in 1940—regional, state, district, and local—was unfavorable. Some, like the people in the villages, were understandably suspicious that there was a trick in such a complete reversal of mill policy. The companies had much to say in their official announcements of sales about giving their workers an opportunity for home ownership with all the attendant virtues of good citizenship: why the sudden conversion to a good American principle they had so long ignored? One leader forthrightly declared and others implied that the mills were unloading a bad investment on the workers, thus voicing the other side of the mill argument that it wished to be rid of the subsidy for village operation. One district leader said that inasmuch as many of the houses were of cheap construction, built in cheap times and with a long period of depreciation behind them, the rents were quite enough for upkeep, and now the mills wanted to sell out at a profit. Almost all union representatives interviewed in 1940 considered the prices too high, though a local leader sometimes excepted a specific sale in his area.

Part of the disapproval centered around their evaluation of the houses the workers were having to buy: they pointed out that many were of light, often flimsy construction with poor sanitation, making them substandard according to modern ideas. This was a period of federal aid to housing and the union leaders felt that the southern textile worker needed, and was as much entitled to, such benefits as anybody in the country. They suggested the creation of local housing authorities which, with government aid, could supply good houses for low rental or for sale on long terms. In this way a double purpose would be served—better housing for the workers and freedom from the undesirable tie-up of job and house.

It should perhaps be pointed out that this suggested solution was somewhat unrealistic. The surrounding public had long accepted mill housing as the mill's business and what it provided as adequate. Certainly its housing compared favorably with much in any specific area. Neither tax payers nor the local public would have supported a movement for federal housing, especially when so influential a group as the mill owners had houses they wished to sell.

Though these labor leaders believed in home ownership in principle, they shared the doubts of social economists after the depression, whether it was wise for low income, mass production workers; they felt it specially unwise for workers attached to an industry subject to such ups and downs as textiles. Their dislike of village sales as a way for workers to achieve home ownership was based not only on what they were having to buy, but on methods and probable results of sales. The suddenness and the pressure to buy because of the housing shortage and the brief time for decision were undesirable conditions under which to make a commitment of this importance. They feared that owning a house so handy to the mill would tie a worker to it more securely than the village institution had done. Certainly during the process of purchase, pay roll deductions, almost universal in prewar sales, seemed likely to tie him there for a period of years.

Naturally part of their disapproval of the sales was relative to its possible negative effects on the right to organize guaranteed by the new federal laws. Home ownership might really do what some managers apparently hoped it would, namely, make the workers more conservative about union activity and especially about striking, thus negating the new freedom and nipping in the bud the rising interest in organizing. Under the new federal laws the control values of the village in this field were limited while the worker still possessed that mobility which is an important asset to the modern industrial wage earner. The freedom to move was, they felt, too high a price to pay for the advantages of home ownership. Especially was this true if the home was a flimsy cottage near a job that was uncertain because a mill's future was precarious or its labor policies unrestrained by a strong union.

It was evident in these opinions that labor and the mills (at least those mills that were selling their houses) had practically exchanged viewpoints. The mills were moving toward the liquidation of the institution they had been defending for decades; labor, which had consistently damned the company village, now preferred it under the protection of the new federal laws to the alternative of buying those particular houses.

Some specific prewar experiences may be of interest. At one organized mill the local union, with the concurrence and advice of their regional officers, boycotted the sale and the company called it off. In a less well-organized area a union leader tried to work out a scheme with two mills contemplating sales. By his plan the union would buy a house a week, hold the title, and let the occupant buy from the union, paying $4.00 a week until it was paid for. If he wanted to sell before finishing payments he would receive a refund of $2.00 for each week he had paid, the other $2.00 being retained by the union as rent, the same rent the mill had been charging. This ingenious plan did not go through. Neither the union man nor the mill managements gave the reason, but it is not hard to guess. The company would hardly be willing to give a union, especially one with which it had no contractual relations, so strong a power over its workers, or, for that matter, so strong a position in the community. One of the mills concerned sold at the time in a more conventional fashion and without opposition. The other waited and, caught with changing conditions of defense and military needs, did not finally make the move until after the war.

In a group of mills where the union was strong but had not yet won a contract, citizens in the adjoining town were under the impression that the union had opposed the sale. Union and management representatives both denied this. However, the union head did say that the announcement of the sale (which was relatively early and the first in its area) had caused great shock to the people. They heard that the company was selling the whole property to an outside party for resale and this added to the consternation. But when they learned the purchaser was a real estate man who had formerly been an official of the mill, and thus known to the workers, they felt better about it. The union officers looked over the contract and liked the prices, rates of payment, and arrangements for financing. They told the management the union would not only not oppose but would approve the sale.

In another group of sales where the union was fairly strong but without a contract, the head of the mills talked over the proposition with the district representative before the sale was announced. Even though the general policy of his union was at the time opposed to sales this representative approved: the houses were somewhat better than average, the prices low, the sale had no definite time limit, and no one had to buy who did not wish to—in fact a decade later the mills still own many houses scattered among the villages. Moreover, the location was in a busy textile area with additional varied industry, thus constituting as little risk for home owning as any worker can hope to have.

Another district representative interviewed in 1940 who was opposed to sales in general said that one mill in his area had made the workers "an attractive offer"—good houses at reasonable prices and on good terms. He was noncommittal about another, but the manager said the union had not entered the picture either as favoring or opposing.

This prewar policy of local union leaders to approve or disapprove depending on the circumstances of the individual sale is well illustrated in sales by two neighboring companies, both under contract with unions. The head of one mill quietly suggested to a few old employees that they could buy their houses if they wished. The news spread gradually and one employee after another came in and "signed up" as they made up their minds to buy. The union never had anything to say about the matter.

In the neighboring company the shock of a sudden announcement and the rush of a definite time-limited sale were further complicated by the fact that the property had been sold to outside parties for resale to the employees. The people were not only surprised at the news but were confused by this unknown element in the situation. It was not made clear to them that this was chiefly a financial device so the company could get the money in a lump sum, and that the sale was "controlled"—conditions specified and closely supervised by the officers and personnel of the company. The union leaders naturally considered it a duty to voice the dissatisfaction of the workers and saw an opportunity to strengthen the young organization in their estimation by helping oppose the sale. The union had had some difficulties with the company preceding its recognition, at which time the National Labor Relations Board had been called in. Therefore, the union turned again to Washington for assistance, and investigators were sent from the Board. The union's appeal to stop the sale as an unfair labor practice was unsuccessful. Most of its efforts were then directed toward getting better terms in general and aiding individual purchasers to have the prices of their houses lowered.

POSTWAR UNION POLICY

When sales were resumed after the war the official position of the unions had become much like the earlier pragmatic attitude of local leaders, namely, for or against specific sales depending on the conditions. Or perhaps it would be more accurate to say that it was to secure the best possible terms in case of a sale, and to protect and assist purchasers after the sale.

A good many things had happened since the start of selling in the mid-1930's to create this attitude and policy. In the first place the sales were going on and there did not seem to be much a union could do to stop them. Federal laws on industrial relations have not, so far, been successfully evoked: it is not a "condition of employment" that a worker must live in a mill house in order to have a job. Possible application of the other side of the coin, that he must work in the mill in order to get and retain a mill house, has not yet been sufficiently tested. A boycott of an individual sale was possible and, as already noted, was employed against one. But a boycott has certain dangers. There is the possibility that union discipline will not be strong enough to enforce it fully, especially in the face of severe housing shortages. A split on the question could very easily wreck a union. Besides, nearly every mill which has sold announced that any houses not taken by occupants or other employees would be sold to outsiders. This meant finding another house in an ever-increasing shortage of houses, or at best renting from the new owner at rates well above the old mill rental and even above the rate of payment.

The rapid increase in real estate prices made the figures set in prewar sales look like bargains for any sort of house, while the rise in wages made payments progressively easier. Thus there was little objection to prices in postwar sales even when they were two or three times as high as before the war. Indeed prices were mentioned as objectionable in only a few sales and were referred to as "good" or "favorable" in several by both union leaders and individual purchasers. The possibility of government-sponsored housing had disappeared in the maelstrom of war and there seemed little chance of its being resumed by postwar Congresses. Only one union official interviewed in 1947-48 referred to the hope of such projects as an alternative to existing mill housing.

Finally, experience of the people who bought mill houses had allayed some of the earlier misgivings of union leaders. Once adjusted to the idea of buying, even when their first feeling of dissatisfaction had been backed by union protests, most purchasers were pleased with the deal whether they sold a house at a profit or improved it as a home. Ownership was not tying the workers to the mill. Instead, it had freed them to accept the increasingly numerous jobs in the vicinity. Union, mill, and employment service officials, citizen observers, individual workers—every sort of person interviewed—testified to the fact that members of house-purchasing families were working in other mills and in other occupations. This varied from place to place according to employment opportunity on the one hand and the wage scale, working conditions, and employee policy of the mill on the other. But the freedom was there for all to feel and to exercise. A change of jobs no longer meant a move for the family.

If home ownership had not increased the interest in unionism in some places, it had not prevented its progress in others. At a few mills where the houses were sold, organizational efforts in progress at the time failed to reach bargaining strength and have declined; in about the same number of instances the union gained a contract after the sale. By the testimony of both union and mill officials the workers' home ownership had not adversely affected union-management relations, and some thought it had improved them.

This study covered 10 postwar sales where there were unions; in 8 the union had a contract. The range of experience will illustrate the union policy of dealing with each sale on its own merits.

In a sale where the union was officially perfectly neutral the manager said the union leaders expressed their personal approval to him of this evidence of the mill's confidence in the workers and its assistance to the people in becoming home owners and better citizens. The workers at the company's other plants, also unionized, were asking to be allowed to buy.

In a second, the president and another member of the management said they heard nothing of a union position, either favoring or opposing the sale, and expressed surprise that unions had been known to oppose them. The union in this company is quite vigorous and has had several strikes and a number of cases before arbitrators. Its lack of action on this question was, therefore, not simply passive acceptance of a new mill policy. The head of the local union said that the announcement of the sale caused some dissatisfaction because the people did not know the prices or the size of the payments. As soon as they learned that the prices were good and the payments no larger than they would be able to pay "on most any rate of wages," they were eager to buy, and the union took no stand. He said that "a good many" of the people who purchased had gone into other work, especially construction which paid higher wages. In this respect the sale had been bad for the union since it meant a loss of these members. But he felt that in the long run the union would profit from home-owning, stable citizens who might return to the mill and to membership in the local.

At a third the manager called in the union officials to tell them about the sale before the announcement. He made it clear he was talking to them as leaders in the community and not as union officers, insisting that the sale was not a bargaining matter since no one was required to live in a mill house in order to have a job. They were among the first to sign up when the sale started. In this case the prices were low, approximating those in prewar sales for houses in good repair with paved streets, connection with the town sewer system, all houses with toilets and most with baths. There are only a few mills in the immediate area, though there are a number some twenty miles away in several directions.

A district union officer whose area included one mill which had sold and others which had not said, as did the management, that the union "had not entered the picture at all." The people had had plenty of warning that the houses would be sold when a program of repair had been completed, the prices were reasonable and terms satisfactory. This was the same village where the announcement of a sale in the late 1930's had been withdrawn, because upon union advice the people simply would not buy. By 1947 this episode was not cited by union officials at a distance and was vaguely disclaimed on the spot by union and management alike. Local people interviewed said "I believe I did hear of something of the kind years ago but it must have been at —————— mill." The favorite one named was a mill which had changed hands in the interim. Everybody seemed satisfied enough about it two years after the sale: few of the purchasers had left the employ of the mill, few houses had changed hands, and many buyers had made improvements. A union member from a neighboring mill regretted that the houses in his village (two, three, four-family and row houses) were not suitable for selling; if they were maybe his company would let the people buy also. The district agent, a long-time textile worker who had come up the ranks of unionism, felt that even the compulsion to buy growing out of the housing shortage was not a bad thing. "A lot of people won't take a step like that unless they have to. Now pretty soon those people will own their homes. I wish I had had to buy." He thought the unions might lose some members as people went into other work; "but textiles is their trade and in a mill area like this sooner or later they will come back to it."

In the fifth case the manager discussed the sale with the union business agent beforehand, giving him information about the prices, terms, etc. The union took no position officially, though some of the union committee members objected and said they would not buy. After getting over the shock of the announcement, however, they changed their minds and were among the first to sign up. The houses here were sold at fairly high prices but are larger than ordinary, are within incorporated limits with full water, sewer, garbage, police, and fire services, and most of the streets are paved or being paved by the mill as part of the sale bargain. The village is so located that values are hardly likely to fall drastically. The company is near other mills and a city with varied employment opportunities. While the work is somewhat heavier than average, the wage scale is above that of most mills. There is a large proportion of long service workers, and, because the mill policy had been to give them preference in securing a house, the occupants at the time of the sale were people who already considered themselves permanent in the community.

At a sixth village, people in the community had the impression that the union had opposed the sale. The manager said the union "did not like it but they made no disturbance." It proved impracticable to locate the union officers but a union member said somewhat grimly that the union did not oppose the sale, and the response of several people interviewed briefly in the village ranged from unenthusiastic to downright unhappy. However, it is only fair to add that at the time of these interviews the sale had just ended and the period of adjustment had hardly begun. The local manager was himself opposed to selling the houses and had to carry out a policy determined at the head office. These two factors may be responsible for the unfavorable reaction to the sale apparent at the time the community was visited.

In the next case in ascending order of union concern, information as to union action was contradictory. The management said that at the first news of the sale people jumped to the conclusion that the mill was going to charge current inflated prices—$5,000 for a house. On this basis the union opposed the sale, and the flurry of excitement resulted in a strike. When the people learned prices and payment terms the opposition collapsed and the strike ended. Union leaders insisted that the strike had been about a wage matter and not the sale. They conceded that the announcement had caused a furor in the village and that the subject was heatedly discussed at union meetings. They explained that the feeling of shock was intensified by the timing. It was soon after the war and many of the people in the houses at the moment had moved in during the period of war operation. They expected to "go back home" later; due to the housing shortage they now had to buy where they had no intention of remaining permanently. Moreover, the type of goods manufactured stood in some danger of being superseded by other fabrics. The workers were uneasy about what reconversion and postwar conditions might do to the mill, or certainly to the jobs as then constituted. The fact that the houses were sold without a general repair seems to have added to the feeling of grievance. The manager said that since this had not been possible, the price on each house had been set with the probable cost of necessary repairs in mind. But the purchasers were very conscious of the money that must soon be expended for repairs; those who were interviewed mentioned this item immediately.

In one postwar sale the union officially raised a series of objections. These included technicalities about the legal status of the selling agent and a challenge that the mill could not give a clear title to the properties being sold; that the company was selling the houses because it intended to close the mill; that prices were too high and the "grace period" part of the contract too stringent. The union's effort to prevent the sale by an injunction failed. The company was able to clear up the technicalities; it pointed out that, far from closing this unit, it was then in the process of moving in more machinery. The grace period of 60 days in case a man lost his job and could not make weekly payments was allowed to stand, but the company agreed to a 20 percent reduction in prices and extended to 6 weeks the month's time for an occupant to decide whether to buy before anyone else, in the usual order of precedence—an unhoused employee and then an outsider—could purchase the house. The union declared it would boycott anyone who bought out from under an occupant. The final outcome was that all were bought by actual occupants or, through exchanges arranged among themselves, by others in mill houses. Thus none was available for purchase by the 50 percent of the employees not housed by the company.

The vigorous action of the union here may have many underlying causes not easily discernible to one unfamiliar with the union-management relations in this particular case. Two obvious factors, however, must have had considerable bearing. The mill is located in an area where unionism is strong, the unions were experienced in protecting their rights and very vigorous in taking up the cudgels for workers with grievances. As in the case of most sales, the announcement was sudden; as has been abundantly shown, this almost always produces a feeling of grievance on the part of the whole group and special grievance by some individuals. Secondly, there are no other mills within commuting distance, so that a home owner here faces the possibility of having to sell at a loss or change his occupation.

In 2 out of the 10 postwar sales where strong unions were present there were no contracts. In one mill a strike to secure a contract was lost and shortly afterward the company announced the sale. It is not surprising that the hard feeling engendered during a somewhat tumultuous strike carried over into this transaction. The company considered that it had unwillingly subsidized the strike through free house rent since the workers had no pay from which to deduct rent. The manager said the union leaders threatened retaliations for what they termed the hardship of the sale. One thing they wanted was cheap rent for the people but he was sure their chief objection grew out of their fear that as home owners the workers would be less interested in unions and strikes. The union workers felt that the company counted on the sale to eliminate the union and the most active members, for although occupants, whether union or not, were given options, "They thought we were down and out because of the long strike and wouldn't have the money for the down payment. But we surprised them—nearly everybody had some war bonds." The union has helped hardship cases to keep up their payments.

The final case involving a union was also complicated by a strike. So far as could be learned, the organization took no particular stand at the time of the sale, and union members, who occupied most of the houses, took up their options to buy. The local had many enthusiastic and active members but had not succeeded in securing a contract. Efforts to secure this resulted, about a year and a half after the sale, in a long but unsuccessful strike. Many of the workers obtained employment in nearby mills. It is highly probable that these jobs were easier to get because they were living in their "own homes," even if not yet fully paid for. Those who had anything like regular work were able to keep up their payments throughout the strike. The union assisted about 100 families with their payments for vary- ing lengths of time during the period.

At the time of the sale some had financed through the building and loan; many of those who started paying directly to the mill have since refinanced through that institution. The union officers said the people liked this better because the building and loan allowed smaller payments over a longer term, freedom to pay as far ahead as one wished, and a less strict grace period if payments could not be met for a while. Besides, they added, less than 20 percent of the houses now furnish workers to the mill. But since the house sale, the mill has changed hands and operations so that it needs far fewer workers. One worker interviewed was of the opinion that under the circum- stances the sale had worked out all right for the mill and the people too. Another said the people were surprised at the time of the sale: "The mill sure took advantage of us, in selling at a time when we *had* to buy." But her cheerful tone belied the words, and her pride in her home was patent. She added, "Everybody likes it fine now and it sure came in mighty well after the strike started."

A state union officer who has had the opportunity to observe many sales at both organized and non-organized mills has thought long and seriously about the problem. His views on sales and their effects form, perhaps, a good summary of the present union point of view. He says the union favors the sales in general because it favors home owning as good American practice and has always disliked the com- pany village. There are some bad features. Besides those already mentioned, he added that many of the villages were poorly planned and will never make really satisfactory residential areas. The mills are selling the houses for as much as they cost, which he considered too high in view of the lack of improvements. Not, he added, that the workers objected to the prices, "but then they have never ob- jected to any prices including those for their labor! But the cotton mill workers are coming up in the world; you can't tell—maybe they will begin to speak up." He was encouraged that the people at a recent sale in his State, though without a union, "kicked" so vigorously at the prices that the sale was almost stopped. Preferable to the sales of many existing villages would be federal housing proj- ects. Pending these a satisfactory substitute, in his opinion, was the policy of some of the newer managements coming to the South in arranging for real estate companies to build the necessary houses for the employees of new plants. In this way the people get good modern housing that is not tied directly to the employer and the job.

This union official concedes that home ownership will make workers more conservative but, for all that, better union members because they will be better citizens. Since they can't be thrown out of their houses they won't be afraid to take part in union affairs and even to strike—witness the last case cited above where, under a difficult situation, the union grew stronger instead of collapsing. It is true that freedom to work at other mills and occupations may cause a given local to lose some of its home-owning members. But they will carry their ideas of unionism with them and will be open to organization at the new job. For example, people who got a taste of collective bargaining at a war plant 50 miles away had helped to educate workers for unionism all over the area when they went back home or scattered after the war. In his opinion the break-up of the mill village will benefit the workers and the community, and in the long run the union and unionism as well.

CHAPTER 9

Results of Sales

THE shift from corporate ownership of many houses as complements of the factory to individual ownership of each house as a home is a fundamental change and has economic, psychological, and social consequences. Some of these can be seen at once; others will be long in emerging. Some are capable of measurement, though so far few have been measured with any real accuracy; others are intangible and are matters of opinion.

EMPLOYERS

No party has such mixed feelings as the employer's group. This is because "the employer" is a composite of many people with many different responsibilities: top management, superintendents and others on the operational level, and personnel workers. The results of the same sale often appear different to each of these groups.

The views of the managers are affected by two conditions. First, they are the men who made the decision to sell. It is only human nature for them to emphasize results which confirm their judgment. Secondly, they quite understandably stress different phases depending on the person to whom they are talking—whether to the representative of a "liberal" university on a social research mission or to a fellow mill man looking for the hard facts upon which to base a similar decision. Thus a few who sounded rather more favorable than otherwise to this interviewer were said by other mill men to be sorry they had sold.

Two managers who sold parts of large villages, one before and one since the war as experiments, considered the results unsatisfactory because of the loss of workers and intended to retain the balance of their houses.[1] The head men of another company were divided in their opinion. A few managers were on the defensive: "We are not sorry we sold," or a little cagey, saying that their particular situation had developed unfavorable features. Two of this noncommittal sort were widely cited by other mill men as quite regretful of the move.

[1]. See footnote p. 25.

A sympathetic but realistic observer who knew their situations well declared that their regret centered partly at least around the fact that they had sold before the war and, therefore, at low price levels. And yet, it was commonly reported in the communities that a combination of the saving on upkeep and the income from the sale had been the means of placing shaky companies back on their feet. The official of a strong company remarked that the houses they sold in the 1930's would now bring two or three times as much "but that is water over the dam, and we are not sorry," even though a good share of the pay roll deductions for the old low price came to the company in high priced times.

But the great majority of managers on the face of it have no reservations as to the wisdom and desirability of the move and many are highly pleased. In general their estimate parallels their reasons for selling and shows that they think the results have fulfilled their expectations: (1) stopped the subsidy on the houses and released funds from that investment; (2) allowed full attention to manufacturing; (3) rid them of a source of annoyance; (4) proved fairer to employees owning or paying high rent outside the village; (5) and converted workers into better citizens and more responsible members of the community.

At a lower level of management, most superintendents and foremen think selling the village was a bad thing. They are haunted by the fear of machines idle for lack of operatives, and are inclined to blame any labor shortage on the sale. They are closer to the workers in the community, and so they view with distaste and occasional alarm the fact that undesirable people buy or rent houses and they no longer have the power to get them out of the neighborhood. Two superintendents went so far as to say they would never take another job where a mill did not own its houses. An occasional superintendent thought it a good thing, and one who had vigorously opposed selling at the time said a year later, "My job is a better job because of this move, less annoyance and a more responsible, self-respecting group of people to work with."

Fewer members of the personnel group were interviewed than of the other two, but from direct and indirect information they seem to be about equally divided as to the impact of the sales on their function. Some say relinquishing ownership of the houses makes recruiting harder: "We have nothing to offer a good prospect"; "All the good workers in the houses work for us and we can't get the poor ones out to replace them with good." The views of others range from no regrets to enthusiasm. They say there was rarely a house vacant for a new worker anyhow; their office is free of the "gripes" about who was to get a house; it is fairer to all in the cost of living.

In regard to certain problems which affect the whole employer group, events during the dozen years since sales began make it impossible to isolate results of the sales from general economic conditions. From about the middle of 1940 onward the increasing demand for labor by the mills was accompanied by ever-increasing competition from other jobs. And yet only four managers definitely blamed their labor shortage on the fact that they no longer had company housing. They all owned a mill or a group of mills close to neighbors who had not sold. Some of the new home owners went to work for their competitors in the labor market. One of these suggested to the other mill in his town that it sell also, probably on the theory that there would then be some take as well as give, but the other manager always smiled and said he was doing very well as it was. A fifth manager lost workers from a partial sale. This mill was entirely on war orders with full labor priorities, but, because the jobs were heavy, the work coarse and fast, the local employment service was unable to send some of its applicants to those jobs, though it was supposed to keep that mill as fully manned as possible. The people simply exercised, or threatened to exercise, their right to take no job at all.

In one company everybody from top management to foremen seemed highly pleased with the results except executives of a unit near a war plant making an exotic new product and provided with full labor priorities. This unit had no priority and it lost some of its home-owning workers to the war plant, but since it also had difficulty getting materials the labor shortage was not as crippling as it might have been.

Most managers were philosophical about the effect of the sale on their labor supply, saying they supposed they got their share in an abnormal situation. During the war a superintendent bemoaned the sale whenever he had a few machines standing idle; the manager reminded him that the mill had been breaking all its records for production. To another superintendent who regretted no longer having the houses for needed workers the manager asked, "Which of our loyal and regular employees would you move out to get a house for the new worker?" since almost every house was still furnishing operatives to the mill. At a village made up chiefly of double houses a large proportion of the purchasers took over the whole house instead of renting half, thus creating a greater than usual housing shortage. And yet the manager said he had fewer machines standing idle for lack of help there than at another plant not far away where the village had not been sold.

A few mills have fairly accurate records of the number of houses still supplying workers. The figures covering some of the prewar sales are as follows:

No. Houses Sold	*No. Now Furnishing Workers*
30	27
170	135
190	150
100	94
71	65
130	113

In several large sales involving from three to a dozen villages the managers said the mill was getting workers from "most" of the houses. On the other hand one personnel worker said the company secured employees from only about half of 150 houses sold; a superintendent estimated that two-thirds of the people in the former 200 mill houses worked elsewhere. A union leader declared that the mills got workers from less than half of the 700-odd houses sold in four villages in his jurisdiction; the report from the mill management was more optimistic.

In the postwar sales the proportion providing workers was naturally much higher. At seven villages where the sale had taken place from 6 months to 2 years previously the houses were furnishing workers just as before; in one, all but 5 houses out of 300 after 2 years. In only two postwar sales had the number fallen off greatly.

Informants at both old and new sales sometimes added that the mill did not get all the workers from the houses. Some accounted for it by better wages which relieved mothers from working or made it possible for young people to continue in school. Mills in or near small cities said young workers seek employment "down town." Girls, in particular, consider stores, beauty shops, and telephone exchanges more attractive than the mill, and in at least one area their preference has contributed to a shortage of spinners.

Whatever effect these sales may have had on labor turnover, the facts are even harder to isolate than on labor supply. War and boom times are always accompanied by more job shifting. The opinion of most managers is that home ownership has stabilized more people than it has set to shifting about within a radius of home base. Figures at hand for one large company seemed to bear this out. For the period 1929 to 1940 annual turnover (quits plus discharges) rates for the entire cotton manufacturing industry ranged from a high of 38 percent to a low of 15 percent. The company's rate followed the national rate very closely, the greatest divergence being 10 points above in one year and 8 points below in another. Its villages were sold in 1941. Beginning that year the annual rate has been far lower than that for the industry as a whole. For example, in 1941 it was 22 percent compared with 43 percent; in 1942, 42 percent compared with 69 percent; in 1943, 52 percent compared with 89 percent.

On the other hand in one area where many mills sold well before the war and many did not, the sales seem to have added to labor turnover. Accurate figures for the scores of mills concerned are not available, but every person interviewed who was in a position to know the situation said there was a great deal of shifting from mill to mill by the home-purchasing workers. Informants connected with mills that had sold naturally viewed this with considerable disfavor and one somewhat bitterly declared that, "A lot of them got jobs away from home just like the one available right at hand so that they could get gasoline allowances." Qualified observers in public-service positions could afford to be more impartial on the subject. They agreed that a lot of the people did jump around from job to job, far more than would have been possible if there had been no sales. But they believed that this large group free to work anywhere kept the mills on their toes as regards wages, working conditions, and treatment of the worker on the job. One official said the improvement in personnel work and practices had been enormous in the area during the last five years; he attributed much of this to the presence of a free-ranging group of home owners. Another public official in the same town thought it was a very good thing for the people to circulate around and thus get out of the isolated pockets of their own mill villages.

Many referred to the factors in the labor supply and labor turnover problems favorable to employer "in the long run" or "under normal conditions." Since the people are now more or less permanent in the vicinity they will eventually come back to the home mill. As one rueful personnel worker said, "In all their job shifting we get a whack at them some of the time." Labor turnover by experienced workers, while annoying, is nothing like as expensive as training green workers. It is probably for this reason that some of the managers who complained most about the purchasers going to other jobs have been careful to make arrangements so that buyers can continue payments rather than having to sell or refinance the mortgage when leaving their employ.

Though the sales program often stirs up suspicions and hard feelings at first, when the shock is over and the adjustment is made, industrial relations are, by the testimony of both management and unions, as good and sometimes better. A superintendent who opposed sales in general and reluctantly admitted that it had worked out pretty well in their case, waxed enthusiastic when discussing the effects of home ownership on his own employees: "We've got the finest group of workers we ever had." A superintendent who favored sales said that after people took over responsibility for house upkeep they were noticeably more conscious of upkeep in the mill, less wasteful of supplies and materials, more careful about breakage. He added with a smile that he did not know how long this new attitude would last.

Four or five volunteered the information that employees had thanked them for the opportunity to own their homes, and in the case of prewar sales "especially at such prices." As mentioned elsewhere, employees in an unsold village were asking to be allowed to buy. Still another manager reported an astonishing experience: the mill reserved nearly a fourth of its small village to have space for expansion and was continuing to rent at the old rates. The workers in these houses told the manager they thought he should increase the rent because "the mill can't come out at these rates."

EMPLOYEES

Many of the ways in which sales affect the workers have been discussed in previous chapters on the cycle of their personal and family response and the reaction by the unions. One problem which permeates this whole adjustment is that of higher living costs. Taxes, insurance, routine upkeep and major repairs are additions; water and lights at regular commercial rates are increases over living in the subsidized village. Textile wages are now at their highest, not only actually, but relative to wages in other industries. It may be that they will retain this relation because of federal laws and actual or potential unionism. But it must be remembered that as late as 1943, when the average weekly earnings of all manufacturing wage earners was $45, those in cotton, silk, and rayon manufacture were still around $25 after a decade of federal efforts and three years of defense and war pressure on the industry.

Another problem relates to ownership versus mobility and to labor turnover from the workers' point of view. The success of modern machine industry is based on the rapid training of workers in a few specialized skills. The interchangeability of parts in the machine is matched by a slower but effective interchangeability of workers. If the worker is not free to change his job or his occupation, or to follow relocation of his job or occupation, he has all the disadvantages and none of the advantages of a system characterized by technological shifts, by economic ebb and flow of his industry and his individual plant. And so, in theory, he should be able to move. Anything that anchors him to one spot may be bad even if, like home owning, it is accepted as good in itself. The anchor in this case may be economic, the risk of having to sacrifice part of his savings by selling at a loss in order to move. It may be psychological, natural inertia, reinforced by affection for that bit of the earth he has made a part of himself.

But practically speaking things work out somewhat differently. Except at the invitation of a gold rush or a war plant people do not move at the drop of a hat even if they own no immovable possessions. When they do move most of them stay fairly close to home base. The "labor supply" of an area is described along with "natural resources" as a permanent attraction for capital investment. Considering the great shifts in kind and location of industry in this country, there are surprisingly few "dead towns," and fewer still which died in less than a generation. The presence of a labor supply attracts new possibilities of employment. The growth and diversification of industry in the South, for example, operated to lessen the possibility of employment vacuums from which people have to move. On the other hand workers adjust to new and changing jobs. The textile operative has done a vast amount of adjusting and learning new skills in the last two decades to meet changes in machinery, fibers and fabrics both within his own plant and among the several mills of concentrated textile areas.

The cotton mill worker, aided by the system of company housing, has had great freedom to move, and he has long been the proverbial mover. But he has always moved within a relatively small circle. The writer has had occasion to interview thousands of new employees of mills; one from more than a county or two away was a rarity. A few mills have mapped the birth places of their working force and found that as high as 90 percent were born within a radius of 25 miles. Ease of transportation has increased the number of workers from farms—from owner families who are at least reasonably well anchored; from tenant families who, as many studies have shown, move short distances.

The indications are that textile workers move less than they used to. As the proportion of workers housed by the mills decreased, textile families have been deterred from moving for lack of a house ready to go along with the new job. As more have housed themselves by ownership or private rental they become free to change jobs within commuting distance. School principals in communities where villages had been sold were asked whether the new ownership had decreased the number of pupils entering and withdrawing on account of family moves. Most said tentatively that it may have; nearly every one of the dozens interviewed added, "We did not have much of that in this community before the sale." Those who had served from 20 to 25 years in a community contrasted the present with conditions in the 1920's on this point.

There are also indications that this greater permanence of residence in the community is accompanied by greater permanence with a given company, through either continuous or intermittent employment. In the last two decades mills have grown increasingly aware of the costs of labor turnover. It is now a concern of top management instead of chiefly a source of inconvenience to superintendents and foremen. Recognition of long-service workers has become fashionable. It takes the form of dinners, clubs, buttons, and pictures in the paper, and occasionally of something more substantial like retirement annuities. Most mills having unions, and some that do not, give vacations with pay, graduated to reward varying lengths of service. Samplings encountered in the course of this study show that even with the increased labor turnover incident to the war it is not uncommon for 40 percent of the working force to have at least five years of continuous service. If intermittent service were counted the proportion of those who are "permanent" in the community would be at least doubled. Intermittent employment has always been a feature of women's and young people's work in the mills.

Labor turnover affects only the minority. For example, a superintendent where the houses were sold eight years earlier said that, for the year 1946, 75 percent of the employees had stayed for the entire year and yet he had some 1500 people on the payroll in order to keep a working force of around 500. In other words, 25 percent of the jobs had been filled on an average of eight times, thus justifying his disgusted remark that some jobs had had dozens of people on them. He said that since the sale, "They mill about too much to get interested in church and community activities." But it is quite possible that these changes could have taken place without a single family concerned making a move.

All these factors suggest that permanence of residence for the mill worker is neither so rare nor so great a handicap as it now sounds in theory, and as it actually was when mills were scattered and furnished the only kind of industrial work in the area. The measure of truth that lies in the depressing axiom, "Once a cotton mill worker, always a cotton mill worker," grew out of complex social and economic reasons of which the company-owned village was only one, though it received much of the blame. With more mills, more different types of employment, and with automobiles, the worker can now get considerable freedom of choice within reach of a permanent home.

This freedom to change both employment and occupation without upsetting the whole social framework of the family group is desirable for the head of the family even though he has pretty well chosen—or circumstances have chosen for him—his line of work. It is even more desirable within the family, for a wife who may have some other skill, for a child who has other tastes and talents. People in the mill villages have always been more realistic than the critics of the system about the company's requirements that all available labor in a house work in the mill if needed. They know why the house was built and why it has been rented at a low rent; they see daily its relationship to machines in operation or standing idle. To be sure they sometimes try to circumvent the system in order to forward the ambition or desires of a member of the family. Sometimes they succeed if the labor needs are not too pressing or if the house still supplies a valuable employee. For example, the head of a group of mills in a city with many and varied employment opportunities said, "Every morning the busses through the villages are filled with people going downtown to work as it is. Where would we be if we sold the houses?"

Where indeed, until the recent changes—shorter hours, better pay, better working conditions, and less obvious huddling of one occupational group into isolated communities—have persisted long enough to overcome the social disesteem of cotton mill work? As a superintendent who struggled with war labor shortages while seeing experienced mill operatives from his former village work downtown at lower wages and longer hours exclaimed, "We've got to glamorize mill work!"

THE COMMUNITY

The American people believe so firmly in home ownership as a foundation for good citizenship that when observers are asked to appraise the effect of the sales on the community they almost unanimously say it has been good: "Naturally makes them more interested"; "They feel more responsible"; "more permanent"; and so on. Insistence on concrete evidence produced some examples. A dozen managers speaking of twice that many former villages said their employees were showing more initiative in starting clubs, group activities, and recreational ventures, and what was more important, in keeping them going. "They used to wait for us to start things and then not take much interest." Such groups frequently ask for and receive mill assistance. Individual villagers told with some enthusiasm of lively clubs, of sociables, of parties to raise money for equipment or charities. Managers of the few companies whose elaborate community programs had survived the depression said their people had always been active in these programs and they saw no difference since the sale.

The churches have long been the most active groups in mill villages. Several kinds of observers such as mill managers, teachers and school principals, community and church workers, cited increased church attendance and interest since the sale, and occasionally the undertaking of a new church or religious education building. The mixing of non-mill with mill families in churches, formerly almost unheard of, was mentioned in a few localities.

The school principals interviewed were, for the most part, in communities where sales took place some years ago. Every one was sure home ownership had made the people more interested in the school; their most frequent evidence for this was larger membership and greater participation in the Parent-Teacher Association. One cited a school of 700 pupils which had 1100 members in the PTA, a group made up about half and half of farm and mill families. Several said this organization had aided in providing new equipment. While admitting this was partially a reflection of the better economic situation, they added that interest in participation had not existed before home ownership gave them a feeling of permanence and of having a real stake in the school. One said that the long-time efforts of his school to set a good example in well-planted and well-cared-for grounds had had little effect until the people bought their homes. Others referred to the effects flowing in the other direction—greater care of school property since the families had taken over the responsibility of repairs at home. One enthusiastic principal said that in his 800-pupil school there had not been a broken windowpane in three months and only about half a dozen in the year since the sale took place, and those "accidental—a ball going where it was not intended."

Social and community workers varied a good deal in their esti-
mates of the effect of the sales. Even in the case of older sales they
often could not point to specific changes that had affected their duties
in the former villages; indeed those who started on their jobs after
the sale was well over often did not know the people had bought
the houses. Upon learning this some thought it accounted for certain
facts they had observed. Illustrative of this is a town with two villages. One village was sold in 1939 and the other has not been sold,
referred to as A and B respectively. No agency person interviewed
except the police knew of the sale. The police saw no difference;
neither A nor B was as bad as their "slum district." The county welfare case worker saw no difference and "They wouldn't tell me they
had anything for fear they would not get as much help." The family
welfare service worker had noticed, and produced figures to prove,
that she had relatively fewer cases of family difficulty coming
from A. She added that the cases were less severe. The Salvation
Army leader had had no calls by needy people from A during the
four years of his service but many from B. He and the YWCA sec-
retary had observed some differences which suggest that the young
people of A are beginning to feel less isolated and "different." The
girls from A come freely to the central YW and take part in the
program, mingling indiscriminately with girls from all parts of
town; group work with those of B still has to be carried on in their
village. Boys from both areas come to the Salvation Army building
where groups, especially for athletics, are organized on a neighborhood basis. Those from A get along better with groups from all parts
of town; those from B have a gang spirit that makes them difficult to
handle, and in contests, a "toughness" that makes them unacceptable
to other neighborhood teams.

Similar suggestions of at least some small changes in community
patterns were to be found in other towns, though it might be a
different agency which had observed the change. For example, the
police in one town said the mill village areas (sold in 1939) had been
practically free from juvenile delinquency in recent years. In another a community worker told with much nostalgia of the welfare
program the mills used to carry on, contrasting it with the dreary
present. Then she took the writer over a small but well arranged
community house and explained its schedule of activity: nursery
school, kindergarten, arts and crafts for children and adults, mothers'
clubs, social clubs, dinners, dances, games, athletics, organized play,
all proceeding briskly on their own initiative with a little paid and
volunteer leadership provided by town and churches.

The evidence of influence of the change to home ownership on local issues and government is likewise uneven. Two former villages have voted to come inside town limits since the sale. Sentiment in most of the others outside town limits was said to be against annexation, often reciprocated by the town or city because of the extra expense that would be involved in providing one or all of such things as water or sewer systems, or paved streets. The villages surrounding Gastonia voted heavily against a move to be taken into the city limits. Some already had full water and sewer systems which had been built by the mills before the sales; others did not have these but felt that the proposed addition was so large that all they would get from annexation would be increased taxes.

Two former villages have set up sanitation districts in order to issue bonds for a water and sewer system. Several others are contemplating this move. One voted for such a district and voted against incorporation as a town. The people of Fieldale, Virginia, accomplished a striking feat in community effort. Under that State's laws the amount of bonds which could have been issued by a sanitation district would have been far too small to install the water and sewer system. Their leaders and representatives of the mill worked out a plan by which the company would pay in cash 75 percent of the total amount needed, this being its part on a tax valuation basis. The people would raise the balance, $300 per household. Within a month every property owner had paid in his money and work began soon after. The village now has its system clear of debt instead of having to pay for it in taxes over a period of years.

In several cases former villages which were already inside town limits have voted strongly in favor of bond issues for schools and streets though they knew it now meant more taxes for them instead of simply for the mill. In two instances involving street and water improvements the six former villages concerned already had these facilities, but as the public officials reporting said, "They seem to be willing to pay their share so other parts of town can have them too."

When asked about interest in politics most observers retired into the clichés about home ownership—"Stands to reason that as tax payers and permanent residents they are more interested now." In four cities informants said theirs had long been "hot political towns" and that the mill people's interest and participation had been lively before the sale as well as since. In one case at the next election after the sale the "outs" attacked the "ins" for accepting the water and sewer system from the mill, saying the mill should have continued to maintain the utilities. The vote supported the officials who made the deal.

In each instance the former village remains an entity recognizable and recognized. Even when it is inside town limits and merges continuously with other residential areas, the style, size, general uniformity and spacing of the houses shows where it begins. By all the evidence it is still a neighborhood made up of the employees of a single employer, bound together by many common bonds of work and long established patterns of community living. A little variety is achieved when some work at the old occupations but for a different employer, more by those who branch out into different occupations, and still more by the gradual seeping into the neighborhood of non-textile families as the houses change hands. So far most employers have viewed all this as a loss of potential workers and as the chief disadvantage of selling a village. A few took it as part of the price of a change which they believed to be sound on both business and social grounds.

This latter view was oftener found among managers new to textiles or new to the South, men not wedded by long usage to the tradition that having a mill village was one of the ways to run a mill. And yet, some striking examples were provided by warp-and-woof southern textile men. A second generation mill man has long felt that the mill people should be mixed up with others; a worker in one of his former villages said, "Yes, some of the folks here work other places. . . . No, the mill doesn't care where people work. They pay good wages and know they can get workers." In a case where more than usual of the resales had been to non-mill people the superintendent could have used workers from those houses, but the chief owner, also a second generation mill man, was proud of the intermixture that was developing. He declared that the former villages were coming to resemble any other suburban area. A new municipal recreation program is bringing these areas into its activities exactly as it is in other parts of the town. An elderly man who had spent his life as part owner and officer of a small mill took the writer along the street to point out houses from which a member of the family worked elsewhere, or which had been bought by a tradesman or mechanic. "They see how other employers treat and pay workers and see that our mill is not so bad after all. They have neighbors who make their living in other ways. It is better that way." Recently an employee had to quit because the neighboring mill had learned he was working here and had notified his family they must vacate the mill house unless he returned. "I don't blame that mill. We would have done the same thing when we owned the houses—had to when we subsidized them. But I don't like that sort of thing. It is regimentation and I don't like regimentation—too much like Germany."

It will take awhile for the former village to be merged into the rest of the community. The changes which the new owners are making in the houses are slowly breaking down the physical uniformity. The old economic and social uniformity is slowly giving way. With new responsibilities and new outlook, even the old political and psychological patterns are beginning to show signs of change.

CHAPTER 10

Some Appraisals of Sales and the Selling Process

IN preceding chapters the emphasis has been on the presentation of facts about mill village sales. Opinions from people concerned with, or close observers of, the sales are part of the "facts" discovered and have been included. Sometimes background material and interpretation have seemed necessary, but evaluations have been kept at a minimum. It is perhaps proper to venture some appraisals of the reasons, the process, and the aftermath of sales.

REASONS FOR SELLING

The socio-economic changes behind the sale of mill villages have not affected all textile firms equally. Therefore, the wisdom of this move can vary from the point of view of the individual mill; it can vary even more from the point of view of the workers, of the community, and, if one may be allowed a somewhat pretentious word, of social justice. In a private property system it is accepted as right and proper that an individual, or a legal-fiction individual like a corporation, can do what it wishes with its own property. And so it is legally right for a company to sell a lot of houses and parcels of land to its workers when its record of regularity of operation is poor and its economic future is uncertain. But workers in general and employees of such a company in particular have enough risks to bear without being compelled to tie up their savings in a gamble where all the odds are against them. The community which has this sort of plant as its main place of employment might well view a sale with some misgivings.

Although two or three groups have had a close shave, so far no sale by an operating company has resulted in the buyers' being left stranded on their little properties. This may well be because of two favorable factors. First, up to the present most villages that have been sold are within easy reach of other mills. One mill was closed after the sale but the people got jobs in the surrounding busy textile area. Second, the increasing activity ever since sales began kept all mills going either by their original owner or some eager buyer. This may not happen in less profitable times. During the depression there

94

were a number of sales of villages by closed or bankrupt mills, but at least the people knew what they were buying.

Some companies showed a sense of responsibility on this score. Several managers said that part of their study before deciding on a sale was directed to the question of steady jobs. Some have apparently not considered this problem. In fairness to the worker-purchasers and the community, it is to be hoped that at least those isolated from other sources of employment will examine their record and prospects before deciding to sell.

On this question of location and its bearing on the decision to sell there was a division of opinion among mill men. Some said they would sell if they were "off by themselves where the home-owning workers could not float off to other mills." Others said that was the worst location in which to sell; some workers were sure to go into other work, and a mill so placed would have no supply of trained textile operatives, or indeed of untrained labor, to fall back on. Again the question of fairness to the home purchaser is of some social interest. His mill may keep running but he, for all the thousand and one reasons that cause workers to leave or get fired, may not have a job there. This makes it desirable for the isolated mill which sells to be doubly sure its policies are fair and just. The same applies to the various units of a company. In an effort to prevent workers from floating from one unit to another they sometimes have rules limiting the hiring of workers from another of its plants. Such rules should probably be re-examined when the workers buy the houses.

The internal situation is quite as important as the location. Many mills have carefully studied the costs of the village, and the resulting figures urge them to sell. Other figures and facts are probably more important, such as working conditions, work load and wage scale. An occasional manager said that part of his confidence in selling lay in the knowledge that his mill would be able to hold or attract workers because its wage scale was better than the average in the vicinity. A few said they had "good running work" or "nice work," the latter usually meaning some specialized type of textiles which had the double advantage of being able to pay better rates and was not quite "cotton mill." Several said their companies had not sold, and one regretted selling, because of the competition of non-mill occupations. Some of these jobs paid more and others less, but the latter were more socially desirable. A company that is unfavorably situated in these respects may need its houses so it can be sure of at least a nucleus of workers.

As to actual wages, it is hardly fair for a mill to sell if it is not paying a wage which makes possible the extra cost of home owning. A few of the prewar sales took place under such conditions, but increasing wages and regularity of work soon improved the situation. For a while this question was somewhat academic, but textile activity has levelled off and the 4-day week and less is re-appearing. If mill wages should drop in relation to their own wartime rates and to other wages and living costs as they did following the first World War, a wage supplement in the form of subsidized housing is a legitimate charge against the industry. However, the fact that few mills house anything like all their workers still leaves the problem of fairness.

A sale is more successful for all concerned if the company has built up a body of permanent employees and if a large percentage of the houses are occupied by this type of worker. Some mills apparently let a needed new recruit rather than an old employee have a house. If the houses are kept for floaters, the policy of option to occupants catches many who will continue to float. Several mills which have had the smallest number of resales and are continuing to get workers from most of the houses reported a long-time policy of giving permanent and valued employees their turn at vacancies in the village.

A few mills in prewar sales reassured their temporarily agitated workers by promising, either directly or indirectly, that those buying the houses would be protected in their jobs or given preference in lay-offs. When jobs became more plentiful and houses scarcer, such promises seem to have disappeared. As these conditions change the temptation may arise to suggest something of the kind again. But this may be a very difficult promise to keep. It would have to be based on more careful selection of both workers and home purchasers than is common. It presupposes cooperation between departments and units of a company and between the employment and production officers more thoroughgoing than most mills have at present. It assumes a willingness on the part of the workers to shift from job to job. While they do this in their own moves and adapt to the gradual modification of their regular jobs, they are often reluctant to make the sudden shifts which might become necessary in juggling jobs and people to fulfill such a promise. Union seniority rules and unemployment compensation reinforce this reluctance. A worker's best protection is the ability of his company to provide steady jobs and a personnel policy that recognizes efficiency and service. If these do not exist and have not already been demonstrated, a pleasant little promise at village sale time will not make it come true.

The advice which every manager who has sold was most willing to pass on to those who have not was "study your own situation." All the above phases of self-examination are but an expansion and this observer's interpretation of that terse piece of wisdom. It is at once the basis for a decision to sell and the first step in preparation for a sale.

PREPARATION FOR A SALE

In this next step the majority made an obvious error in tactics and a lapse in simple human kindness as well: a sudden announcement of the sale. Some managers who admitted they had been considering the move, studying and preparing for it for years, sprang it as a surprise. A few cases were encountered—and there may have been more—where the presence of surveyors running the lines for the lots was explained as for some other purpose. By now there have been so many sales so widely scattered that this piece of business will no longer prove a mystery. At future sales the villagers will be assured of a short warning at least when this begins.

There are concrete advantages in announcing the policy before-hand. The people can prepare for their down payment. They can do their house swapping beforehand. A little of this goes on during the village sale, and a few instances were cited of exchanges involving three or even four houses. But with the agitated feeling usually accompanying a sale, it is not easy for families wanting to make exchanges to get together quickly, to say nothing of weighing differences in price, size, lot, location, etc. Anything more than a simple swap between two tenants is something of a *tour de force*. To be sure the permission to make exchanges at sale time has psychological value in that it gives a feeling of choice. That it is impractical is shown by the small number of exchanges then as compared with the large number during the payment period when they are more trouble to the mill, to the financing agency, and to the inexperienced real estate owner.

An early announcement would give those who do not want to buy a chance to arrange an exchange with a non-housed employee who does want to buy. In the few sales where the houses were sold in batches, all after the first had this advantage, as of course all did in the gradual sales. An excellent example of such an adjustment comes from one of the gradual sales. An employee of 35 years standing still occupied the six-room house he had when his family was large. The manager suggested that he and his wife take a smaller house. But he had lived there so long he considered it home and would not agree to move. When, in the housing shortage, the question came up again the man was so upset that the manager said, "All right, you don't have to move. I won't ever mention it again." During the next year or so more and more of the employees bought their houses, and this man devised a way to stay in "his home." He got a son-in-law, a non-company-housed employee of the mill, to buy the house and let him live on with the family.

The greatest advantage in an early warning is, of course, in industrial relations. It is human nature to be against any sudden change. Writers on personnel matters in the textile trade papers are constantly reminding the mills that their custom of "posting notices" of changes is poor practice for that reason. An edict announcing a change with as many ramifications as this for the worker automatically arouses antagonism and suspicion. Many instances have been cited in other connections where the shock has, at least temporarily, disturbed employee relations.

Sales experience indicated that tenants made better adjustment to the idea when the houses were in good condition. Lower prices in lieu of repairs does not have the same effect, since the purchaser is all too conscious of the impending expense. Many mills after deciding to sell put on a special program of repair. If they had announced this decision, they would have received a double benefit: a longer warning to the people and the psychological effect on them. One mill included in the study did this with very good results.

If utilities such as water and electricity are to be changed over to a public system it would seem desirable to have it done before the sale. The people then become accustomed to regular commercial rates and to paying the bill instead of the too easy system of having it taken out of their pay. This is especially true if these services have been on flat rates. At the low, and often nominal, charges which many mills make for the non-metered water and electricity people get into habits which are extravagant and wasteful. They have to learn to use these items more carefully. Even without a village sale, when a mill has put in meters and has begun charging in proportion to use, though at less than regular commercial rates, the people are amazed at the size of their first bills. As one manager said somewhat facetiously: "The ditches were full of cheap electrical apparatus when they saw how much current they were using." In several instances the coincidence of this change with the sale added yet another difficulty to the adjustments that had to be made all at once. In a few of the sales soon after the war the scarcity of meters made it impossible to make the change earlier. Occasionally a mill has had to continue the old system until facilities could be provided and an arrangement worked out with the town or utility company. While this may not seem so desirable to the mill, it does have the advantage of allowing for adjustment to one thing at a time.

The timing of a sale may cause irritation and even a feeling of injustice, as, for instance, just before summer vacation. One company announced its sale very shortly before Christmas. There were features in this case which in other sales have been the basis for unfavorable reaction by the people, but these were minimized here, all but eclipsed in the general feeling that it was "mean to pick a time like that." Fears about reconversion or a postwar slump made workers feel that the time selected was bad, though subsequent events dispelled this uneasiness. Local reasons for fearing short-time operation, temporary shut-down or lay-off are reflected in the fact that workers, both organized and unorganized, rather frequently complain that the "grace period" is too brief and try to get it extended. Conditions of this kind may well become an important factor in timing sales in the future.

One manager said this postwar period is a bad time to sell for the following reasons. If the prices are low the people will not be able to resist the offers of quick profits and presently many of the houses will be either rented to them at higher rates or occupied by non-mill workers. In the latter case employees will be pushed farther and farther from the mill with consequent problems of transportation and absenteeism in bad weather. If the prices are in line with present values and the general level of prices and earnings should go down, the people will be disgruntled and feel that the mill has "done" them, and some might even lose their homes. A number of other managers who sold before the war or had not sold at all voiced similar opinions.

The initial announcement of a sale is usually a letter to each occupant telling him he may buy. It bears the marks of having been carefully formulated and doubtless each sentence has been weighed in lengthy conferences. It is the personal opinion of the writer that much of this care is love's labors lost. If there has been no inkling of the move beforehand, the chief thing the reader gets out of the letter is that within 30 days he must buy this house at an unknown price on unknown terms or someone else will buy it. The rest, including generalized phrases about good bargains and easy terms, just does not soak in. Sometimes an especially altruistic phrase about the opportunity the company is offering or about the joys and virtues of home owning prompts a cynical response. The workers know why a company is selling. Scores of them encountered casually and interviewed briefly were asked, "Why do you suppose the company decided to sell?" Some gave several reasons, but the first response was almost invariably, "To get rid of the expense of the village, I reckon."

The gap between the time of getting the letter and learning the price and terms is the critical period. Then rumors abound and dissatisfactions arise. A manager who had one of the best planned and most satisfactory sales encountered in this study said that, so far as he knew, the only mistake he made was in not putting the price of each house in the letter to its occupant. He sensed instantly the need for this and within 24 hours was giving that information to all who asked for it. One company did put the price in the initial letter.

Some have bridged this gap successfully by discussing the whole plan with union officers, a move which has much tactical merit. These officers can help explain the conditions, and their leadership is strengthened by the confidence instead of their being embarrassed by a surprise. One company gathered the employees at the community house where the local agent managing the sale explained the whole plan. Another selected workers, considered by the foremen to be representative of the departments, to meet with the specialized selling agent to hear details and ask questions. In this case the most prominent questions are illuminating: "Can I sell if I want to?" "Can anybody sell to a Negro?" "How will we be treated if we own our homes?" "Will I have a job?" In one large company a rumor got out that a sale might be in the offing. The community workers were besieged with questions and much embarrassed at being unable to answer them. The chief of this staff went to the head of the mill for clarification. The latter then called in the teachers, preachers, community workers, and leaders and explained the whole plan so that all would be in a position to answer questions.

THE PROCESS OF SELLING

Nearly every manager was inclined to think the machinery he used for handling the sale—directly by the mill, by a local real estate agency, by a specialized selling agent—was the best way to do it. This happy state of affairs is not very illuminating to the student or to the mill man contemplating a sale.

For the small company a sale run by the mill itself takes advantage of the close, face-to-face contacts which commonly exist between the employees and the head of such a mill. Some very successful sales have been carried on by "the boss" himself. In one case, for example, the people came in as they decided to buy over a period of five years, and the chief executive had time for this business along with his other duties. Another mill manager arranged to devote practically full time to the project for the necessary period; he was a good salesman selling fair houses at low prices in an area with much industry, and he finished up the job in a few weeks. In several others the head of the mill deputized a member of the organization or hired an outsider to help in seeing the people and handling technical matters but with easy access to the top men in the company. Several large sales over a relatively short period have been conducted in this way with no great hardship to the executive concerned and with much on the credit side in close relations at a crucial time. Any of these methods make it fairly easy to do some selecting if there are some families to whom the house will not be offered.

Sales conducted by local real estate agents or by building and loan associations also lend themselves to a period as extended as seems desirable. Representatives of the agency know local conditions and property values. They are familiar with the policies of the company, its reputation among its workers, and with at least some of the people. They can, and often do, finance the mortgages and receive the payments. Because of the size of the job or for local tactical reasons the work was occasionally divided among two or more agencies either according to their personnel available or by letting the purchaser choose whichever agency offered terms he preferred.

In early sales, or first sales in an area, local agencies have sometimes been reluctant to take on these projects which were as strange to them as to the workers. They are now increasingly willing to do so. The movement away from pay roll deductions means that a local institution must handle payments, transfers, sales and the like, for the next five to ten years; it might prefer to do the whole job. There is a distinct advantage in public relations in letting the local people have the business. It was suggested that if they had it from the beginning there might be less of one bad feature, the constant dangling of offers to resell. Many managers as well as others in the community complain that "Somebody is after the people all the time. All they want is the money they can make out of this rising market." The record on this point is inconclusive: sales that were handled locally are among both the highest and the lowest in resales.

Sales conducted by agents specializing in such operations have the advantage of efficiency, a point of considerable advantage in a large sale. It is the assembly line come to the real estate business. The agency has only to convince the management, or often just one man, whom conditions and laws and cost figures have helped to convince already. The rest is routine. Their personnel is experienced in the various phases of service which a company may wish to use: appraising, manning the selling office, interviewing in the homes, financing or arranging the financing, paper work connected with the sale. The well-nigh universal testimony was that they "do a bang-up job."

But even some managers who used this system could see certain disadvantages. Their comments, the observations of managers who studied and decided against this method, and the reaction of workers make it possible to summarize some of the weaknesses.

It is a disadvantage to have strangers interposed between the workers and the mill managerial group at such a time. This has been minimized in some sales by having members of the latter easily available or taking an active part in the sale. And yet one superintendent was glad outsiders were running the sale; even so the people wanted to pin him down about job preferences, and he felt they would have been more insistent if he had been actively managing the deal. Another disadvantage could be avoided by a little frankness. The purchasers often have the idea that the agency gets a large commission: "at least 10 percent," "all our down payment," "a big rake-off" that makes the house cost more. With their small experience in such matters they do not realize the complexities involved and wonder why such an agent should make a lot "just for 'selling' to us when we have to buy." A few managers who had agreed to make certain repairs after the sale said, "You have to watch out or they will promise too much." Others pointed out that since the commission was a percentage of the price, "They naturally are interested in as good a price as possible." It should be noted, however, that in sales where a specialized agent was employed prices were quite comparable to those managed by the mill itself or by local agencies.

The chief disadvantage is a by-product of the specialization and the efficiency. Such an agent wants—indeed is obliged—to get the job done with a good deal of dispatch. The pressure of a time limit is almost necessarily added to the pressure of circumstances. Occupants who are slow to make up their minds are told how many other people are asking to buy those very houses. Numerous instances of this were encountered, including that of a woman who bought against her better judgment because, "They kept telling me about somebody else who wanted this house." At this sale the management had definitely said no one had to buy who did not want to—that particular house would not be sold. However, she was uneasy and her aged parents, long-service employees, did not want to move. Presently sickness and the loss of a wage-earning son made the payments difficult and the idea of the mortgage worrisome. She appealed to the head of the mill and he bought it back, refunding what she had paid and more due to rising prices; he gave her the assurance she needed most, namely that she could have the house as long as her parents wanted it.

The time limit, almost a necessity with an outside agency, is also a common feature however the sale is managed. Enough has been said in other connections to make clear its disadvantages. Most of the undesirable features grow out of the combination of a sudden announcement and a short time limit. In a few sales where the policy was announced well ahead the customary 30 days were not needed. It is only fair, and good industrial relations besides, for the people to have more time either before or after the sale is definitely announced. The mill village is a southern institution with well over a half century of history; its roots and traditions are older still. Its operation and effects have been a part of the life of textile workers for their lifetime and that of their parents. It is a little out of proportion to close it out in 30 days.

The almost universal practice of offering the houses to the occupants has the virtue of simplicity and convenience. In the present housing shortage it also has practicality on its side. It recognizes the status quo. When the status quo is good the results are usually good. Some mills actually have long had a policy of selecting tenants for the qualities which southern mills claim they have in mind in making up their working force and their communities. Some have not done this and so at sale time there are inevitable disadvantages to this rule of thumb. Some buy who do not want to; it is probably this group who resell so readily. Certainly among these is the occasional occupant who, through a subterfuge, sells his option to an outsider. Also some get houses who do not "deserve" the chance under the avowed principle that the mill is giving an opportunity to good workers and good citizens. A few mills had the temerity to do a little selecting at the time—refusing to offer the houses to some families. But under a general principle of option to the occupant this can hardly be done except in the case of those so patently "undesirable" that they understand the reasons and the neighbors tacitly endorse the action. Otherwise, with a housing shortage and a quick sale, the whole group of workers would be thrown into confusion and uncertainty.

In addition, there is the employee who has been paying high private rent. He has already been discriminated against by higher living costs as compared with his fellow worker in a company house. And all through no fault of his own: lack of enough company houses, accident rather than length or quality of service, or, as he may feel, downright favoritism in assigning the houses. With a sale this discrimination is compounded by an opportunity to buy at prices well below those current in the area and on terms favorable to a purchaser with little cash or credit. It would not be strange if those left out in the cold were resentful. And yet this investigator found no evidence of such sentiments. No manager, worker, or union leader mentioned this as one of the problems, and a good many who were directly questioned on this point said they had heard no reflections of such a feeling. The people are practical enough to realize that in a change of this kind everything cannot be perfect for everybody.

The greatest virtue of the option to occupants and then to other employees is that it places the houses directly and immediately in the hands of the workers. In this respect the housing shortage has reinforced a policy that is good for mill, worker, and community. The secondary condition set up by many, that houses not taken by the employees would be sold to outsiders, has had little opportunity to become effective. The majority are holding on to their houses; many of those who sell, sell to other workers for occupancy. So far, even in the oldest sales, the percentage that have become rental property is small.

If the movement to sell villages continues, the advantages to the employer are such that this policy of option to the occupant will probably be followed by new sellers. It is to be hoped that it will be. The defects pointed out above could be, and in some sales have been, avoided; they are relatively minor compared with the undesirable features that would follow wholesale disposition for rental purposes. A couple of managers said they had had offers to buy the whole group of houses at more than the prices set for the sale to employees. Several more said that local real estate or financial interests had made blanket offers to buy any not taken by the employees, or to take any employee-purchaser's house off his hands at an advance in price. While this enthusiasm may stem from hope of a profit on a rising market, it contains a possibility of large rental holdings. If the mill worker is going to be a tenant of a landlord who has anything approaching a monopoly he is better off if that landlord has an interest in him as a worker greater than the interest as a tenant.

The history of housing in some of the New England textile cities furnishes a clue to what could happen. As mill housing declined in the larger centers private capital took over the task of supplying tenements. By the turn of the century slum conditions had developed with poor upkeep, bad sanitation, rents sensitive to rises in wages but insensitive to declines, and overcrowding. Between 1900 and the first World War several cities found it necessary to make official investigations and take measures to ameliorate conditions. In the smaller communities company housing for part of the working force lingered until recently. During the 1930's many mills so situated disposed of their houses by auction sales. While this did not insure purchase by occupants, housing and economic conditions at the time meant they had no great competition in bidding; financing was often arranged to help them buy.

Southern textile history has recapitulated much of that in New England. The mills, the people, and the communities will be fortunate if the dissolving of the village system can profit by that experience and avoid the ills of the larger centers. Auction sales are not feasible as a means of disposing of the southern mill villages. Under present conditions the people would be far outbidden and have either no houses or high rents. The two early sales which were nominally by auction were actually pre-arranged sales to employees.

Incidentally it is interesting to note that at no sale was there mention of a higher price to non-employees. Before the war a sprinkling of houses, and since then an occasional one, was sold to outsiders for residence or for rent. It is rather to be expected, with the emphasis most mills have placed on the low prices it was offering to its employees, that some would have set up such a differential.

The relatively few mills which have sold only to those who wish to buy and as they wish to buy reaped benefits in easy adjustment and in the building of a good permanent working force. This method recommends itself for future sales. The obvious disadvantage is that the company may be left for some time with part of the village on its hands and with property scattered all about the village. But nearly all reserved some houses for key men—and those who did not, regretted it—so that they have houses to take care of. Moreover, the majority are obliged to continue some village services and quite as many find it good employee relations to continue aid and counsel. Hardly a one has cut loose from the village immediately following a sale. And so this method involves problems different only in degree rather than in kind.

The amity surrounding one such sale as compared with that of a neighbor's quick, complete sale has already been cited. In another which followed this plan, the management had no regrets for the patchiness of its property holdings or the prolongation of sale and house care. The superintendent here favored home ownership and sales in principle but saw many possible dangers: you might need the houses to secure workers; you might get undesirable people buying the houses; you couldn't control the situation. He added, however, that nearly a decade after the sale none of those dire theoretical contingencies has developed, "though they may yet." His home owning workers are regular, responsible, and cooperative: "When you want a little extra work done in the mill it is one of the home purchasers who is willing to do it." All this was at a time when many mills were complaining that high wages and the passing of war psychology were resulting in much absenteeism. He was acquainted with sales of the "take it or leave it" sort and strongly condemned the hard-boiled tactics used in some sales: "It is just too rough on people."

As was made clear in Chapter 4, prices have varied less than might have been expected. Within the two distinct price levels of the pre-war and postwar sales the average and the modal prices have by no means reflected the difference in the nominal bases used in setting prices, in local conditions, nor in value. Superficially it might be supposed this was due to the employment of specialized agents in many sales so that the prices they have helped to set became a pattern. But some where they were influential were among the lowest and among the highest both in dollar price and in value; and so also were those set completely by local agencies. Usually where the price was below average the management considered a "generous price" as good labor policy.

The chief flaw in this general uniformity of prices is that the people are buying such different things for very nearly the same money. Some examples will illustrate this. In a prewar sale, substantial stucco houses, with plastered walls and double floors and full baths, on paved streets inside city limits sold for only about $100 to $200 more than those of light frame construction, ceiled, on long, leggy pillars with no underpinnings, a water tap on the porch, and dirt streets, at a mill well outside city limits. Neat four and five-room bungalows with bath, on well-graded or naturally level lots with space for good-sized gardens of one village sold for within $100 to $200 of the price of those at a mill not far away where the three and four-room, old, flimsy cottages were perched on lots so steep that, as one resident expressed it, "You'd have to level off a place in the back for the dog to sit on to howl," no gardens, a pump at the corner, and the main road, unpaved and clayey, plunged down a steep hill. The same is true of postwar sales. In several instances excellent houses with water and sewer connections and with paved streets and side-walks sold for actually less than houses that were no better in vil-lages with none of these expensive installations and so located that they cannot easily connect with any existing system. Such property owners face the problem of incorporation or organization of some sort and heavy expense before they achieve the services that are not only convenient but are almost essential where people live close to-gether.

It is not so much that the poor buys were not "worth" the usually modest price but that others got so much more for the same money. Of course this kind of group difference in value is more apparent to the observer of many sales than to the purchasers. The latter are much more concerned with differences between houses in their own village.

Certainly the prices of all except a very few have been favorable to the workers. All the "busy work" that went into finding a basis —tax or fire insurance valuation, a percentage of value or replace-ment and the like—boiled down essentially to a search for an amount they could afford to pay in weekly or monthly installments and would not be too great an increase over former mill rent. Several managers said frankly that this was their main consideration in de-ciding on the general price average. Since textile wages are fairly uniform and mill rents low, the resulting price works out to similar figures. This formula produces prices which compare favorably with the commonly accepted standard for investment in a home. Accord-ing to this rule 2 years' income for a home is excellent, 2½ to 3 possible, and 4 too much. The majority of these purchasers have signed up to pay an amount equal to about 1 year's wage of one worker, though of course interest during the payment period raises the total to near 1½ times. Even the highest priced, except for a few double houses the extra half of which is virtually self-liquidating, cost considerably less than 2 years' wages for one worker. Before the war at sales visited during the first confused feelings, people would cite hardship cases. "Look at John S————, he can't buy his house [for about $800]. He is the only one working, making $15 a week, and he has five children and a sick wife." Well, he could not really afford a dollar a week mill rental. Even the village system was not cheap enough for one not very skilled worker with a minimum wage and a maximum family. It is perhaps a cruel fact that no change can be so cushioned that it will work no hardship on the weakest or least fortunate members. If it does not press too hard on the general average, that is perhaps as much as can be expected in this workaday world.

The average employee before the war could manage it on wages he was then getting, and as his payments proceeded he received a progressive reduction in the form of increased wages, regular work, over-time, and jobs for all members of the family who could work. The postwar buyers will not be so fortunate if the reverse process sets in before they have acquired sufficient equity in the house to enable them to refinance the balance on longer, lower payments. For this reason it was well that the 8 and 10-year terms common in prewar sales were almost entirely abandoned in favor of the 6 and a fraction-year term; the 5-year plan of one large group of mills which sold shortly before the war would have been better still. In the future, the danger of short time may make a longer payment period desirable. All plans make it possible to pay faster and some mills encourage this in positive fashion. In view of the uncertainties of the future they might well do more in this line.

The chief advantage of mill financing grows out of the economics of the textile industry and of its housing traditions. In the few early sales which encountered short time or temporary shutdowns those mills ceased the deductions for pay as smoothly and naturally as many customarily cease those for rent under similar conditions. Many deferred payments for an individual or two in cases of sickness. The next decade may witness conditions under which deferment would be highly desirable. One mill man even suggested that under extreme conditions the mill could cancel the balances due, since most villages have been pretty well depreciated. This also would be well within the paternalistic tradition, would keep the trained workers in the vicinity, and save them the demoralizing shock of losing their homes and becoming tenants of outside landlords. Such a move might be a great deal easier if it involved eschewing an anticipated income instead of making a cash outlay for the balance to the financing agency.

The rather general shift to outside financing and direct payments by the purchaser to the agency has, however, many advantages over the mill carrying the mortgage and deducting the payments from wages. The company can thus get the proceeds in a lump sum large enough to be useful in improvements, though in some they did not get even this advantage since the arrangement was to receive the money as it was paid in. Experience has shown that the deduction system, while it may help to hold some employees during the payment period, is by no means certain in this respect. When it does not hold them there is the trouble of collections by the mill or refinancing by the purchaser. While pay-roll deduction is not as distasteful to the mill worker as outsiders think it ought to be—witness the number who elect this method when they have a choice—its psychology is on the negative side. The responsibility for meeting an obligation regularly and voluntarily has apparently proved to be good training for the new property owners.

AFTER THE SALE

Enough has been said about the advice and aid in such matters as upkeep to indicate that most managers have been helpful in seeing the new home owners through the period of readjustment. On such post-sale problems as resale, refinancing for a longer payment period, or remortgaging the property to get cash, many expressed regret about individual cases in their former villages. Except in unusual circumstances they felt that these moves were unwise and unjustifiable. They advised against it when they had an opportunity but admitted that they either did not know about it in time or were afraid the advice would be received as interference.

And yet, at least one manager was very successful in this field. He sold the villages in 1938. In the early 1940's he became concerned about rumors that "the real estate boys were after them" with offers at large advances over the original mill price. He addressed a communication to purchasers of the houses, reminding them that, if they sold in a rising market, they would have to buy in it, and that in his opinion, "This real estate situation is getting dangerous." He had no repercussions: "They knew I was interested in them and was giving them the best advice I could." And they followed it; very few houses have been sold in the decade since the original sale and those chiefly by people actually moving from the area and to other employees of the company. In this case there were evidences of excellent industrial and personal relations between management and workers. It is likely that wherever such mutual confidence exists the management could have offered unsolicited advice without having it misinterpreted or suspected.

That some such effort is worth making is shown by the experience in another sale. Here 60 percent of the houses have changed hands, many several times and always at increased prices. A number are now rented at rates representing a return on an investment of three times the village sale prices. When asked what would happen if decreased income made these rents impossible to the mill workers, the manager said the owners would have to reduce the rents, a move which they would make most reluctantly because of their actual cash investment. Here the effect on mill and workers will not be great because the number of houses involved is not large. But it does give an insight into the problem when a large proportion of the workers are dependent for housing on what was formerly the mill village. Such conditions would leave the workers a choice of paying high rent, accepting poor upkeep, or seeking houses farther and farther from their work place. As previously quoted, this last contingency has prevented some mills from selling. The union at a mill that has been under contract for a decade offered some figures on this subject. A survey made in 1938, the year the houses were sold, showed that 90 percent of the union members lived within two miles of the town and 75 percent within two miles of the mill itself. In 1947, 60 percent lived at least five miles away and many fifteen and twenty miles.

The tendency for welfare work to be continued more or less as before a sale is a sound decision, both to avoid additional sudden change and to preserve the values it may have been creating in the community. Since few companies which sold had elaborate community programs, the majority of the home purchasing workers are more affected by the fairly common practice of aiding employee-initiated groups. These activities represent real interest and participation by the people. Each case can be judged on its own merits, rising or falling according to its own vitality instead of becoming institutionalized, as some welfare programs do, and hanging on whether there is much life in them or not.

It may be objected that in this way the employer can still control much community activity by his selection of the groups he aids. But experience indicates that he is usually willing to assist any sort of group except unions, and their policy is to avoid subsidy anyway. It may be further objected that continuance of welfare programs or even company aid to worker-initiated groups is still paternalism and has no place among self-respecting citizens. But many a company in all sorts of industries which never had villages has long considered aid to, and even paid leadership for, employees' activities worthwhile. When there is no housing to raise the question of controls, such programs usually have not been the butt of cynical criticism.

For despite the cries of paternalism, the institution of work creates bonds between employer and employee which go beyond the exchange of work and wages. One of these bonds is mutual interest in local community affairs. It finds expression, especially in small towns, in the acceptability of leadership from among the various ranks of management. To be sure, the day of the mill owners' houses on the nearest hill has just about passed. His successors, top management, now dwell in suburbs along with other people of similar social and economic status. But the superintendent usually, and the foremen generally, live in the village. After a sale they still do, either because the company reserves houses for them or they buy as other employees do. Current trends toward the recruiting of potential foremen and other production executives from among technically trained young men may change this situation. For the present, however, most foremen and many superintendents in southern textiles are men who rose from the ranks. The qualities that won their promotion make them leaders in the community. Many a textile community is a better place in which to live because of the activity of these natural leaders outside the mill. Their effectiveness in community affairs is due, on the one hand, to their place in the managerial hierarchy, and on the other to their being part and parcel of the people.

A few cases were encountered in this study where a community was deprived of these leaders by the sale of the village. The mills concerned offered for sale the houses of superintendents and foremen along with the others. Since the company was no longer going to be furnishing them substantial houses at low rent, they seized the opportunity to buy houses in the adjoining city. They, like the upper management a generation earlier, preferred to invest in houses and live in neighborhoods with people of similar economic standing. According to the testimony of community workers whose duties and observations cover the entire city and its suburbs, the former village areas are the poorer for this loss. In one case the union is providing some leadership; since the area is largely inside city limits, politics may gradually help to develop leaders in this field.

The managements that have sold their houses are naturally interested in the results because of the effect on their workers in numbers and quality, in attitude and character. They are also interested in the outcome of what is for each something of an experiment. And so they keep themselves informed. Granting all that, one cannot help being impressed by the detailed knowledge the majority have of the former village. They are proud of the success not only for the mill but for the people. They describe—or take the visitor around to show off—improvements with as much satisfaction as their predecessors in the heydey of welfare work used to show off a community building.

These men accept as a by-product of the new order the fact that they will not be able to "control" any labor in the economic sense of requiring operatives in exchange for furnishing houses. While a disadvantage in the last few years, under different conditions of the labor market they may find it a source of satisfaction and of strength that the families of their employees have one or more members with other resources. One of the many depressing features of the company town in any industry is the fact that short time or a shutdown means that everybody in the community is on short rations. In textiles, the long tradition of housing and paternalism, by their very existence, helps to weaken a mill's position in a declining market. The employer puts off reducing production beyond the dictates of good business—the hard-boiled one lest his experienced employee-tenants move too far for recall, the humane one for the additional reason of hesitating to precipitate hardship on a group so completely dependent upon him. He runs on a slim margin or actually in the red. He cuts prices, depressing the market still more or nipping in the bud any little boomlet, in his eagerness to get orders in his highly competitive industry. He cuts wages, or institutes a share the work system, four days, three days, work for the whole force. The village is not the whole reason, but its family employment system, its landlord-tenant, employer-worker interdependence has increased the precariousness of an industry famous for ups and downs. Unemployment compensation will make reduction in force possible without too great hardship; because of its availability unions are insisting on layoff according to seniority rather than excessive decrease in weekly hours. If to this is added a more varied employment base the result will be beneficial to all.

Incidentally this frank use of the word "control" by mill men is of interest to the long-time student of the mill village. Twenty years ago when controls were strong and criticism of the village system was lively, this writer never heard them use the word. They shied away from it even when they were describing, proudly or defensively, the very things that made for control. Now they use it quite freely in the economic sense referred to above of a labor supply in return for subsidized houses. They even use it in the social and moral sense of being able to eject undesirable people from the community. A few consider the loss of this latter kind of control a disadvantage of village sales, especially as related to bootleggers who are, actually or euphemistically, the archetype of the undesirable. The majority of those who have sold, however, seem to have arrived at the conclusion that they do not wish to have, or to exercise, this kind of control.

One index of this change is the disappearance of "private property" signs in the villages. Twenty years ago these were common on roads and streets entering the village. Hundreds of villages, sold and unsold, were visited in connection with this study: just one such sign was encountered.

Southern mill men know they are operating in a different day from their predecessors: the economic situation, the educational status of the workers, laws affecting industrial relations and wages, the possibility or actuality of unionism—all of these make a new setting. Many of them are adapting their policies to the new day.

THE SALES AND THE LOCAL PUBLIC

A village sale is a venture in public as well as industrial relations. The first aspect is, of course, news of the event itself. The local newspapers usually feature the sale with all the company's carefully formulated statements about the opportunity it is offering to its workers. The editor often adds his own comments on the virtues of home ownership and the contributions that it will make to the community and to citizenship. Once the operation is over some have forgot all about it. They publish local news items as happening in such-and-such a mill village just exactly as before. In at least one town the editor has made a point of avoiding the old nomenclature for identifying persons and sections of the town.

The numerous citizens interviewed in the course of this study may not be strictly typical of the whole surrounding public: those were sought out who had reason or opportunity to observe the situation. But certainly their opinions are based on more than traditional attitudes and have more weight in local discussions of both the process and the results of sales. It must be admitted that an occasional one regards the mill people as a class with characteristics which will continue to make them different and socially distinct from other kinds of working people. Such a one showed regret for the passing of the old controls and old paternalism. Principals of schools, in particular, showed a wide range in their attitudes: downright touchiness at questions about change which implied the village institution had ever set the people apart; apprehension lest there be an infiltration of undesirables; fears for the future under less favorable economic conditions; vague claims of improvement growing out of home owner-ship; firm belief, backed by concrete examples, in increased citizen responsibility.

But the majority of these "outside" witnesses approve of village sales: in detail, such as preference to occupants, price and terms, though they often criticize the suddenness and speed; and in principle because of their faith in home ownership. They, like the employer, have kept an interested eye on the situation and the response of the purchasers has confirmed that faith. These observers show that they have moved away from the old southern acceptance of an isolated, self-contained community for one occupational group. These men and women, both because of their official positions and their insight, can be extremely useful in helping to weld these peripheral areas into the larger community.

CONCLUSION: A NOTE ON SIGNIFICANCE

The conditions which created the southern cotton mill village—made it first a prime necessity and then a desirable adjunct and finally a sort of bad habit—have changed. The virtual cessation of village building 25 years ago was a symptom of some of the earlier changes. The move to sell is based on even more vital changes in the last decade. The rate of sales may slacken for some special reason, as it did during the war years. But it is difficult to believe that the trend will reverse itself completely.

Whether the company mill village passes rapidly or slowly the accompanying adjustments will affect the whole textile manufactur-ing area: employer, worker, village, adjoining town, county, even the labor supply for other industries.

The most obvious will be the change in appearance. But while varied painting and building of extra rooms and changing of details will overcome some of the monotony in appearance, they will not eliminate it. The monotony is more fundamental than these things. It springs primarily from uniformity in size of houses and lots. These will remain for a long time to come. Anyhow, perhaps this physical monotony has been too much emphasized and complained of in a nation with cities full of row houses and suburbs full of housing "de-velopments."

The real monotony of the mill village has been ingrained in its life rather than its houses. The people are all of the same stock, the same cultural background with closely similar religions, of about the same educational attainments and economic level. They all work on the same product at tasks all comprehend and many are experienced in. They are all subject to the ups and downs of the same erratic market and of the same company. The policies of the same management irritate or satisfy them *en masse*. It is homogeneity run riot.

Now there will be a possibility of variety. As some of the purchasers sell the houses, people of other occupations are seeping in: the butcher, the baker, the electrician, the auto mechanic, the plumber— all those who serve the community as well as workers in nearby industries seeking inexpensive housing. Members of mill families will drift into other occupations. Many of them have worked at other jobs already during depression and war and will find the transition easy. The rising generation, especially those with decided tastes or talents for other work, will break away from the mill. From these different jobs they will bring to their homes and their community new interests, new contacts, new relationships with the larger community. All these factors operating in the former mill village will help to break down the monotony that has made its life dull, the separatism that has made it a thing apart.

If there is really any foundation to the American belief in home ownership as a stimulus to more active citizenship it bids fair to be demonstrated in these villages. They constitute a virgin field for the operation of certain social and civic forces hitherto practically absent. One of these is pride in their homes, which shows itself promptly and has persisted at least as long as the oldest sale. Another is social control by public opinion. There are indications that it takes a while for the people to get used to the fact that they can no longer fall back on the mill to control unruly children or anti-social families. Allied to this is the preservation of local law and order. Company police or county deputies paid by the company will be replaced by democratically controlled guardianship. A village policeman said, "I sure hope this mill doesn't sell its houses. It would make my job lots harder." It would eliminate his job as it is now constituted. The offender against law and morals will have to be dealt with, not by firing him from his job, but by due process of law as they are in other communities. Finally, there is the taxpaying citizen's demand for a return for his contribution. This responsibility will come more gradually as the mill ceases to carry on functions that sooner or later must be a public responsibility—streets, lights, sanitation, local community services.

Villages adjoining towns will come into their corporate limits; those out by themselves will apply for municipal charters as Draper, North Carolina, for example, has done. Then will be ended the anachronism of "towns" of 2,000, 5,000, 10,000 people without the means for a part in local government except through the clumsy machinery of the county. Then they will have their own machinery for local democratic control whether they use it for that end or for political wire-pulling and bossism. The people will have to learn the ways of self-government rapidly, just as they are now learning rapidly the ways of home ownership.

The communities around the mills have a stake and a challenge in the revolutionary changes which the sale of the villages implies. They approve the sales, indeed are even more sentimental than the mill men about the virtues of a fuller citizenship and more vocal in their belief that "it will make a better community." Will they also be willing to see to it that the people whom they have considered apart and inferior really share in the larger community in all its ramifications? Will they be willing to sit back and watch the precincts that were once mill village hold the political balance of power and even out-vote them? Will they help to educate the people in citizenship or exploit their political inexperience? Will they be willing to accept them as other workers are accepted and not as "those people?" Will they help, through their financial institutions, by individual assistance, by education and by governmental backing, to see that too many of the houses do not fall into a few hands, with consequent problems of high rents, overcrowding, and slum conditions?

The liquidation of the cotton mill village is the most recent important step which the textile industry has taken in bringing the South into line with the rest of the country. The first was the building of the industry itself. This showed that the agricultural South could manufacture. That the South concentrated its energies too exclusively in that one industry is not the fault of the mills. The second was the revolution to catch up with progress in industrial engineering—call it scientific management, machine efficiency, job realignment, or the stretch-out as you will. The mistakes in this were many and were the fault of the mills: the changes were often made too rapidly and without proper preparation. But through this modernization a great industry weathered its own and the national depression and emerged equal to its task in the war without the aid of government-built plants. This third step is social, psychological, and political. The mill village institution was a fusing of the tradition of the cotton industry in England and New England with that of the southern plantation, slave-tenancy, paternalistic exploitation. It has affected the pattern of other industry in the South. Its necessity and desirability have long since passed. For though it taught the people gathered from farm and mountain the rudiments of community living, progress in these lessons has long since run up against the blank wall of company ownership with its inevitable controls, its limitations to personal initiative, to social freedom, and to political independence. When a "mill hand's" house is his own castle instead of an appendage to his machine, when his community is his own responsibility instead of an extension of the mill management, then shall we have a new experiment in democracy in the South.

APPENDICES

Purpose, Method, and Limitations

PURPOSE

THIS study was undertaken for several reasons. The movement it describes is one among many changes going on in the South. Thus it lies within the province which is a specialty of the Institute for Research in Social Science. The break-up of the mill village is a part of regional, social, and textile history and an example of social change in progress. In addition, I, personally, had three reasons for making the study. I wanted to observe the latest development in an institution and an industry in which I have worked and of which I have long been a student. I wished to bring to my teaching of a course in the industrial community an example of current significance. Finally, I hope the report will be of some practical value. If managements planning to sell see the strong and weak points in the experience of others they may be able to improve their own procedures. Any contribution toward softening the blow and easing the painful process of rapid change to the thousands of families who may become involved is well worth the effort expended. It is, no doubt, too ambitious to hope that the study will have any effect on attitudes and action of the local public surrounding these sales. This public is already interested in the process of sales and the effects on the village and villagers. It is less clearly aware that the change is going to affect the whole community and that the whole community has a part in the readjustment.

METHOD

The original plan envisioned coverage of all sales. This proved to be impracticable. Lists of sales provided by trade papers, associations, and by local selling agents, gleaned from newspapers and made up during my own brief survey in 1940[1] were supplemented by local information. Mill men themselves were the best source of information of sales in their neighborhood, and indeed at a distance as well, because of personal and business ties. However, in areas with

---

1. Reported in articles in *Textile World*, May and June, 1940.

many mills where selling started early or was common, they some-times thought a company had sold which had not, or overlooked one that had. In such areas a further check was made at the county of-fices of Register of Deeds, tax collector, etc. Even so, a few sales by operating companies were missed. The search did discover some 25 cases where houses were sold separately at the closing or sale of the mill itself. While these present a different problem, they do mean, if operations were or are ever resumed, that there is one more mill with no village. They also mean that a minimum of 2,500 more houses are now in the hands of individual workers instead of cor-porate employers. In many communities these represent sizeable ad-ditions to the growing number of textile workers who own homes through their own initiative or with the encouragement and aid of their employers. In areas with fewer mills or where sales started late, the news value of the event usually made it known in a wide radius. Unfortunately not always: a few missed in the visit to their locality were later cited but were then so far away that it was impracticable to back-track.

The sales upon which data were secured included such a range in type of mill, locality, method and time of sale, etc., that complete cov-erage would probably have revealed no important additional find-ings. And yet every sale had its own peculiarities, its own incidents and reactions; in the last one visited a few quirks were found that had not been encountered before. That will probably be true of the next hundred sales and the next.

The proportion of mills that have sold their villages, referred to in Chapter 2, is only an approximation since for such comparison the exact number of sales would be needed. A generally accepted def-inition of what constitutes a sale would also be helpful. Shall we in-clude partial sales? There were two such undertaken for experi-mental purposes and four others where selling was ended before all houses were disposed of because of changing labor conditions just prior to the war. However, the experiences in these cases were val-uable for comparison, and the managements had the same problems of continuing services as if they had sold the whole village. These six were included.

Shall we include those sales referred to above which took place at the time of liquidation or sale of a mill? The present operating company is, as far as labor supply is concerned, in the same posi-tion as those managements which sold their houses and continued to operate. But the new management had no responsibility for their sale nor for the continuation of village services any more than if it had bought a building that never had had any dwelling property attached to it. The relations of mill, houses, and workers are like those where workers built or bought homes outside the village. These were, therefore, not included in the total sales. However, seven cases were included where the mill changed hands after the sale and either the old company or the new continued to collect the payments and provide certain services.

On the other side of the comparison, what mills should be counted in the total? Only those which have villages? No accurate count of these has ever been made. Shall we include in the total all hosiery mills from Virginia to Alabama because three were discovered among the mills selling? But the one hosiery mill included in this study is a unit of a company made up mostly of cotton mills; another, not covered, was converted from a cotton mill years ago and the houses continued to be rented to employees; at the third, the houses were in the nature of a separate investment of the chief owner of the mill though rented mainly to employees. Few hosiery mills have villages and so this type of establishment was left out of the total. Dyeing and finishing establishments are often merely separate plants of cotton mill companies with the same policy regarding housing; separate finishing companies have largely followed the same custom. Therefore these plants are included in the base figure.

Finally, the most recent data on the number of establishments that is authoritative and similar for all States are for 1939, from the Decennial Census of 1940. For purposes of comparing the number of sales with the number of mills these figures are quite satisfactory. That year is near the middle of the period since the beginning of sales in 1934. By 1939 recovery had progressed to the point that most mills closed by the depression had been put back into operation, while few were added during the next six years due to war restrictions on building.

NO. OF ESTABLISHMENTS	VA.	N.C.	S.C.	GA.	ALA.	TOTAL
Cotton Mfg.						
Broad woven goods	10	128	140	81	50	409
Yarn	0	198	18	38	23	277
Thread	0	5	0	3	1	9
Rayon, Broad woven goods . .	10	29	14	3	0	56
Dyeing & Finishing	5	20	10	8	6	49
Total	25	380	182	133	80	800
No. that have sold villages	4	83	21	17	2	127
Percentage	16.0	21.8	11.5	12.8	2.5	15.9

In 1939 the five States, Virginia, North Carolina, South Carolina, Georgia, and Alabama, had 800 establishments in the types of textiles which usually have housing for employees. By states and kind of mills the situation is shown in the table on p. 123.

The mill management was naturally the chief source of data on the actual sale. An interview was always sought with the top man in the company. Industry in general and textiles in particular are wary of investigators, and the policy-making head wants to know who is asking what questions; he usually wants to answer them himself. This habit of the industry suited this investigator especially well in one respect and less well in another. I wanted to know the whys, wherefores, and results of policies; no one else can discuss them as knowledgeably and no one else will discuss them as freely. On the other hand, the head man is a busy person and it takes a long time to secure the factual details. Sometimes he called on another official for specific data; about half sent me to superintendents, personnel men, local selling agents and the like, to secure further details.

Managers who have not sold were asked for their views on the movement and their reasons for not joining in it. Some of these were visited on erroneous information that they had sold. Their reasons for not doing so often centered around concrete difficulty of location as it would affect either the mill or the workers; a few said they did not think their workers would like to buy. Others who have not sold were visited as representative of opinion in the industry and as old friends whom I have called upon for information so many times that I could feel confident of frank discussions.

The somewhat casual nature of this "control group" may be unsatisfactory to social scientists; I have been familiar with the arguments and attitudes of the industry so long that to me, at least, it seemed sufficient.

Any reader of the report is already aware of the wide variety of persons who were interviewed besides those connected with the mill management. Workers and their families encountered on the streets, in stores, gathered at the mill gate for the next shift, and visited in their homes were almost invariably willing to talk about the sale. Where there was a union, local officials were interviewed; in two cases where they were not available rank and file workers were asked for the union attitude. Store and filling station keepers serving the village had observations on both immediate and long-time effects. School principals and teachers, social and community workers, and local officials of all sorts were interviewed. While some of these "outside" witnesses were sought in the vicinity of all sales, a special effort was made at varied coverage at the older sales.

LIMITATIONS

The study has certain weaknesses of which the writer is fully aware. For one thing, the anonymity is clumsy and tiresome. The report would have been easier to write and more illuminating to the reader if I could have labeled every experience or incident with the name of the company. Some of the managers would have been willing for me to do this or at least willing in connection with certain items; fully half definitely asked that their data not be identified. Compliance with this request was necessary, not only as a courtesy but as an encouragement to frankness, and in some instances (especially at branch plants), to gathering the information at all. The listing of mills that have sold in Appendix III is not subject to this limitation. A sale of real estate is a matter of public record.

Another weakness is the scarcity of actual statistics. A manager often had to go to some trouble to secure so simple a figure as the number of houses sold. Figures on the exact number of purchasers who had paid out, were ahead, or behind in payments, or had resold involved more difficulty even if the mill financed the sale. They were quite unprocurable if some other agency handled financing and payments. An occasional manager could furnish some or all of these. In the smaller plants his knowledge about such matters had all the earmarks of practical working accuracy; in the larger mills the superintendent or some other official had this knowledge. But this sort of information did not produce tabulatable figures.

Many phases of the study report opinions and attitudes. Social phenomena of this kind are now being examined with the aid of intricate techniques. Their application involves an intensiveness and presupposes resources far beyond the compass of this survey. And so opinions and attitudes are included though they may be reported inadequately and certainly are given without scientific measurement. But they are the background, the motivation, and even can be the controlling force in the progress of this chapter of social change.

Some Factors in Sales: Typical Examples

In each case a house priced at about the average for that particular village was chosen. In the postwar examples payments and prices are both averages, since the full data were not at the mill offices.

PREWAR SALES

Former Mill Rent: Weekly	Payment on House: Weekly or Monthly	Taxes and Insurance Included	Price of House	Down Payment	Plan and Method of Payment
$ .80	$ 2.48 W	Yes	$ 800.00	0	8 yr. FHA schedule; pay roll deduction
1.00	2.50 W	No	1,000.00	0	10 yr. 1% a month; pay roll deduction
1.00	10.00 M	Yes	800.00	10%	7 yrs. B&L first; mill 2nd mortgage; pay roll deduction
2.00	2.70 W	Yes	900.00	$25–$100 as able	10 yrs. $3.03 per $1,000 balance; pay roll deduction
2.00	12.97 M	No	783.00	10%	5 yrs. pay at various local financing agencies
1.40 to 2.00*	2.89 W	No	1,076.00	10%	6⅔ yr.; pay roll deduction
1.00	2.87 W	Yes	880.00	10%	6⅔ yrs. $3.75 per $1,000 balance; pay roll deduction
1.00 to 2.00*	9.00 W	Yes	1,000.00	10% (but not less than $100)	139 mos. 1% a month; mill carrying but pay at bank
1.00	2.63 W	Yes	925.00	0	10 yrs. FHA schedule; pay roll deduction
1.20	1.55 W	Yes	700.00	10%	10 yrs. pay roll deduction

*Rents raised to fifty cents a room a week just before sale.

POSTWAR SALES

Former Mill Rent: Weekly	Payment on House: Weekly or Monthly	Taxes and Insurance Included	Price of House	Down Payment	Plan and Method of Payment
$1.00	$16.00 M	No	$1,700.00	10–15%	6⅔ B&L and pay there
1.20	16.80 M	No	2,000.00	10–15%	6⅔ B&L and pay there
2.00	18.00 M	?	1,500.00	$25–$100	6⅔ B&L first and mill second mortgage; pay at B&L
2.00	4.00 W	No	1,100.00	0	6⅔ B&L and bank; pay there
2.00	5.00 W	?	1,800.00	10%	6⅔ Investment Co., pay there
1.20	10.00 to 12.00 M	?	1,200.00	Varied	6⅔ Investment Co., mail in
1.20	16.00 to 20.00 M	?	2,400.00	Varied	6⅔ Investment Co., mail in
1.50	20.00 M	No	2,400.00	10%	6⅔ B&L first and mill second mortgage, pay at B&L
2.00	6.00 W	Yes	2,000.00	10%	6⅔ mill carrying; separate office for collection
2.00	6.00 W	Yes	1,800.00	10%	6⅔ mill carrying; separate office for collection
1.30	10.00 M	No	2,500.00	20%	10 yrs. sold to real estate Co., has office for collection

Mills Which Have Sold Villages

THE following list includes all mills for which information as to village sales has been secured from authoritative sources. The latter include, beside personal visits by the writer to the mills, news reports published in *Textile Bulletin* or *Textile World;* the Hugh Pinnix Realty Company, Greensboro, N. C., lists of sales conducted by the company; list of sales prepared by Mrs. Mildred Barnwell Andrews, Committee Representative, Textile Committee on Public Relations, on file with Henry Lesesne of the Textile Information Service.

No claim is made that this is a complete catalog. A few sales were missed by the writer for reasons explained in Appendix I. Unless such a sale appeared in the above sources it was omitted here. A number discovered through local information, visited and included have not appeared in any of these sources. Gradual sales, in particular, rarely get into the news and on lists. Therefore it seems quite likely that List C, sales since the field work for this study ended, is also incomplete.

In a movement currently in progress even a complete tally would no longer be complete by the time it appeared in print. The following list does give some idea of the wide geographic distribution of sales. To those familiar with the industry, for whom it may be of practical value, it also shows the wide range in size, type of product, ownership, etc.

Sales marked with an asterisk (*) are those upon which information is included in this study. Gradual sales are listed in the period in which they began though they may have extended into the next.

A. SALES, 1934-1941
   *Burlington Mills Corporation
      Blue Ridge Rayon Mills, Alta Vista, Va.
      Cascade Rayon Mills, Mooresville, N. C.
      Central Falls Manufacturing Company, Central Falls, N. C.
      Newton Rayon Mills, Inc., Newton, N. C.
      Ossipee Weaving Company, Ossipee, N. C.

Piedmont Heights, Burlington, N. C.
    (houses for several mills)
Puritan Weaving Company, Fayetteville, N. C.
Radford Weaving Company, Radford, Va.
*Cleveland Cloth Mills, Shelby, N. C.
*Drayton Mills, Spartanburg, S. C.
*The Elmore Corporation, Spindale, N. C.
*Esther Mills Company, Shelby, N. C.
*Fieldcrest Mills
  2 mills at Fieldale, Va.
  2 mills at Draper, N. C.
  2 mills at Leaksville, N. C.
  4 mills at Spray, N. C.
*Firestone Textile Mills, Inc., Gastonia, N. C.
  (sale of part of village)
*Gastonia Combed Yarn Corporation, Gastonia, N. C.
*Gastonia Mercerizing Company, Gastonia, N. C.
*Gastonia Processing Company, Gastonia, N. C.
*Gastonia Thread Corporation, Gastonia, N. C.
*Groves Thread Company, Inc., Gastonia, N. C.
  2 mills near Gastonia
Henderson Cotton Mills, Henderson, N. C.
  2 mills
*Judson Mills, Greenville, S. C.
*Laurens Cotton Mills, Laurens, S. C.
*Mid-State Cloth Mills, Red Springs, N. C.
*Modena Mills, Gastonia, N. C.
  (now, Burlington Mills Corporation)
Monarch Mill, Dallas, N. C.
*Pacelot Manufacturing Company, Gainsville, Ga.
*Pacific Mills, Columbia, S. C.
  4 mills
*Pickett Cotton Mills, Inc., High Point, N. C.
*Ranlo Manufacturing Company, Gastonia, N. C.
  1 mill at Gastonia
  1 mill at Ranlo
  (now, Burlington Mills Corporation)
Robbins Cotton Mill, Robbins, N. C.
*Royal Cotton Mill Company, Wake Forest, N. C.
*Shuford Mills, Inc.
  2 mills at Granite Falls, N. C.
  2 mills at Hickory, N. C.

*A. M. Smyre Manufacturing Company
  1 mill at Dallas, N. C.
  1 mill at Ranlo, N. C.
*Spray Cotton Mills, Spray, N. C.
*The Stead & Miller Company, Concord, N. C.
  (part of village)
*Textiles, Inc., Gastonia, N. C.
  14 mills in and near Gastonia
*Whitney Mills, Spartanburg, S. C.
  (closed January, 1946)

B. SALES, 1942 TO EARLY 1948

*Aleo Manufacturing Company, Rockingham, N. C.
Asheville Cotton Mills, Asheville, N. C.
*Athens Manufacturing Company, Athens, Ga.
*Burlington Mills Corporation
  Cramerton Mills, Cramerton, N. C.
  Lakedale Mills, Fayetteville, N. C.
  Robeson Textiles, Inc., St. Pauls, N. C.
  St. Pauls Rayon Mills, St. Pauls, N. C.
  Smithfield Manufacturing Company, Smithfield, N. C.
  Vamoco Mills Company, Franklinton, N. C.
*Calloway Mills
  7 mills at Lagrange, Ga.
  1 mill at Manchester, Ga.
  1 mill at Milstead, Ga.
*Columbia Mills Company, Columbia, S. C.
*Dallas Manufacturing Company, Huntsville, Ala.
*Erwin Cotton Mills Company, Durham, N. C.
  (part of village serving three plants)
Excelsior Mills, Union, S. C.
*Gaffney Manufacturing Company, Gaffney, S. C.
*The Kendall Company
  Mollohon Plant, Newberry, S. C.
*La France Industries
  Blue Ridge Yarn Mills, Pendleton, S. C.
  Pendleton Manufacturing Company, La France, S. C.
*Newberry Textile Mills, Newberry, S. C.
*The Stead & Miller Company, Concord, N. C.
  (balance of village)
*Textron Southern, Inc., Cordova, Ala.

Tolar, Hart & Holt Mills, Inc., Fayetteville, N. C.
*United States Rubber Company
   3 mills at Hogansville, Ga.
   1 mill at Winnsboro, S. C.

C. SALES REPORTED IN *TEXTILE BULLETIN* AND *TEXTILE WORLD* SINCE FIELD WORK FOR STUDY ENDED (LATE 1948 AND FIRST HALF 1949)

Beacon Manufacturing Company, Swannanoa, N. C.
Burlington Mills Corporation
   Oxford Cotton Mills, Oxford, N. C.
   Phenix Mills, Kings Mountain, N. C.
   Steele Mills, Rockingham, N. C.
Dunean Mills, Greenville, S. C.
Lily Mills, Shelby, N. C.
Mansfield Mills, Inc., Lumberton, N. C.
Orr Cotton Mills, Anderson, S. C.
Republic Cotton Mills, Great Falls, S. C.

Index